the
bean

book

the bean book

over 70 recipes using beans and other pulses

hamlyn

First published in 2001
by Hamlyn
a division of Octopus Publishing Group Ltd
2–4 Heron Quays, London E14 4JP

Copyright © 2001 Octopus Publishing Group Ltd

ISBN 0 600 60377 6

A CIP catalogue record for this book is available in the British Library

Printed and bound in China

10 9 8 7 6 5 4 3 2 1

NOTES

1. Standard level spoon measurements are used in all recipes.
   1 tablespoon = one 15 ml spoon
   1 teaspoon = one 5 ml spoon

2. Both metric and imperial measurements are given for the recipes. Use one set of measurements only, not a mixture of both.

3. Measurements for canned food are given as a standard metric equivalent.

4. Eggs should be large unless otherwise stated. The Department of Health advises that eggs should not be consumed raw. This book contains some dishes made with raw or lightly cooked eggs. It is prudent for more vulnerable people, such as pregnant and nursing mothers, invalids, the elderly, babies and young children, to avoid dishes made with uncooked or lightly cooked eggs. Once prepared, these dishes should be kept refrigerated and used promptly.

5. Milk should be full-fat unless otherwise stated.

6. Fresh herbs should be used unless otherwise stated. If unavailable, use dried herbs as an alternative but halve the quantities stated.

7. Pepper should be freshly ground black pepper unless otherwise stated.

8. Ovens should be preheated to the specified temperature. If using a fan-assisted oven, follow the manufacturer's instructions for adjusting the time and temperature. Grills should also be preheated.

9. This book includes dishes made with nuts and nut derivatives. It is advisable for readers with known allergic reactions to nuts and nut derivatives and those who may be potentially vulnerable to these allergies, such as pregnant and nursing mothers, invalids, the elderly, babies, and children, to avoid dishes made with nuts and nut oils. It is also prudent to check the labels of pre-prepared ingredients for the possible inclusion of nut derivatives.

10. Vegetarians should look for the 'V' symbol on cheese to ensure that it is made with vegetarian rennet. There are vegetarian forms of Parmesan, feta, Cheddar, Cheshire, Red Leicester, dolcelatte and many goats' cheeses, among others.

Contents

Introduction

The term 'bean' is used for both the edible seeds and the seed-bearing pods of various plants (called legumes) belonging to the family Leguminosae. Bean seeds, peas and lentils are often referred to as pulses.

Bean seeds (usually dried) and bean pods (usually fresh) are readily available. They come in a huge range of shapes, colours and sizes and are popular worldwide. Each region has its favourite way of using them – falafel and hummus in the Middle East, refried beans in Latin America, dhals in India, bean and pasta soups in Italy, cassoulet in France, pork and bean stews in Eastern Europe. Beans can be served simply, as a side dish, or made into thick soups, stews and casseroles; they can be puréed or mashed for use in dips and pâtés, or served cold, freshly cooked and marinated, in a substantial salad, a meal in itself.

Brief history

Legumes are among the oldest food crops grown by man. Besides being of nutritional value, they are useful in agriculture for their nitrogen-fixing properties, restoring the soil after use.

The preference for specific beans in various countries today derives largely from the history of their cultivation. Bean varieties have travelled widely since, however, and most are now available worldwide.

Broad beans are the oldest-known podded vegetable in Europe and the Middle East, and have been grown and eaten throughout the region since the Bronze Age. The word 'bean' on its own originally referred to the broad bean; only when other varieties were introduced from the New World did 'broad' become necessary to distinguish it from other species. Despite being a staple food for the poorer masses, the broad bean has had some strange and superstitious beliefs attached to it by various cultures, including an association with death and the supernatural. This may in some part be due to the bean's ability to affect some people with a form of poisoning called favism (*see page 9*).

Varieties of beans belonging to the botanical genus *Phaseolus*, native to Central and South America, were introduced to Europe from the 14th century onwards. The haricot bean, first cultivated by the Aztecs, includes a large group of different varieties of green beans and their seeds (*see Haricot bean, page 10*). (The name 'haricot' is a French corruption of the Aztec word, *ayacotl*.) These fresh and dried beans overtook the native broad bean in popularity. Runner beans came later and were initially grown in Europe for their showy flowers rather than as a vegetable. Other legumes with a long history include chickpeas, lentils – their cultivation dates as far back as

6750BC in Iraq – and the soya bean in China – the first written record of which dates back to 2838BC. From China, soya bean cultivation spread to Japan and then to Europe in the 17th century. Here, unlike in the East where soya beans are processed into many different products, the dried beans were initially cooked like other beans and quickly disregarded as unpalatable. Western interest in the bean was revived only when its extraordinary nutritive value was scientifically confirmed in the 19th century. Since then scientists and manufacturers have developed a wide variety of soya bean products (*see page 13*).

Nutrition and health

Beans, especially dried ones, are highly nutritious and account for the origin of the expression to be 'full of beans', meaning to be lively.

All dried pulses, with the exception of soya beans, have a very similar nutritional content. They are rich in protein, carbohydrate and dietary fibre, and low in fat, which is mostly unsaturated. They also supply useful amounts of minerals and vitamins: calcium, iron, phosphorous, magnesium and some B vitamins. Fresh beans have a different nutritional value because of their high water content. They contain vitamins A and C, but these vitamins decrease once the beans have been picked and are virtually lost from

dried beans. However, many dried pulses – for example aduki beans, chickpeas, whole lentils, mung and soya beans – can be sprouted, which makes them rich in both B and C vitamins. Canned and frozen beans retain about half their original vitamin C content.

Dried pulses, except soya beans, contain a higher percentage of protein (about 20 per cent) than most other plant foods. However, this protein is 'incomplete' or 'second class' and needs to be combined with other foods, ideally grains, that complement their various amino acids to produce a 'complete' or 'first-class' protein with the full complement of amino acids required by the body. The ideal combination of pulses and grains seems to have evolved naturally in meals around the world – for example tortillas and refried beans, dhal and chapatis, baked beans on toast. In this way, dried beans are an excellent source of protein for vegetarians and those living in regions where protein is scarce or expensive.

Soya beans have a very high protein content (about 35 per cent), which is more than other bean proteins, and accounts for its nutritional importance – especially in regions where little meat is eaten. Unlike other beans, the soya bean also has a high fat content (about 20 per cent) – used to produce soya bean oil – and is low in carbohydrates.

Nutritional values

Typical nutritional breakdown for dried navy beans (used in canned baked beans) and dried soya beans per 100 g (3½ oz) dried beans.

	protein	fat	carbohydrate	fibre	iron	calcium
navy beans	22.3 g	1.3 g	50.7 g	24.4 g	6.4 mg	155 mg
soya beans	36.5 g	19.9 g	30.1 g	9.3 g	15.7 mg	277 mg

Source: USDA Nutrient Database

Toxins in beans

Dried beans must be prepared properly as they contain lectin, a toxin that is rendered harmless only during the soaking and cooking processes. In particular, it is not safe to eat raw or undercooked kidney and soya beans.

Red kidney beans contain a toxin in their skins, which can be destroyed by cooking the beans initially at a high temperature, making them completely safe to eat. Canned kidney beans are precooked and safe to use as they are.

Soya beans also require careful cooking. They should be soaked for 8–12 hours, drained and rinsed then covered with fresh water and brought to the boil. Soya beans should be boiled for the first hour of cooking. They can then be simmered for the remaining 2–3 hours that it takes to cook them. Processed soya products are quite safe to use.

Flatulence

Dried pulses are well known for causing flatulence, thanks to the oligosaccharides they contain. These complex sugars are indigestible by normal stomach enzymes and so pass into the lower intestine where they are fermented by friendly bacteria, resulting in a build-up of gas. Changing the soaking water two or three times improves the digestibility of dried pulses as the sugars that cause flatulence leach into the soaking liquid. The addition of a pinch of aniseed, caraway, cumin, dill or fennel seeds to the cooking water is also thought to counteract the problem.

Favism

Broad beans are known to provoke a severe allergic reaction called favism in a small group of people of Mediterranean or Middle Eastern origin – the regions where the bean originated. Favism can result in anaemia, physical weakness and jaundice and is thought to be hereditary.

Varieties and Identification

There are two broad categories of beans – those with edible pods (generally available as fresh beans) and those whose seeds only are edible (mostly available as dried beans, but sometimes fresh). Some beans, for example lima beans and broad beans, can be found in both fresh and dried form. Common names of beans can be very confusing, for the same names are often used for different varieties in different countries.

Green bean

This general term covers various fresh beans that have long, edible flat or rounded pods, with small seeds inside. Some beans are skinny, others are much thicker. The pods are usually green although there are purple and pale yellow varieties, too. Most green beans are originally from the New World, and many of these are types of haricot bean. The names are used interchangeably: French bean; haricot vert; bobby bean; runner bean; string bean (originally named for the fibrous indigestible string that ran down the pod's seam, but not generally found now in commercial species); snap bean; and wax bean, a pale yellow variety of green bean. The purple-podded beans look different while raw, but the pods turn green when cooked.

Green beans are also readily available frozen or canned. Frozen beans, particularly, are a good alternative to fresh.

Lima bean

This bean is named after the capital of Peru, from where cultivation spread slowly northward and to Africa and Asia. There are two distinct varieties – the fordhook and the smaller sieva. Lima beans are popular in the USA, where they are usually sold shelled and frozen, or fresh in their pods, which should be plump, firm and dark green. Although young lima beans do not require shelling, they usually are shelled just before cooking to reveal plump, pale green seeds with a slight kidney-shaped curve. Lima beans are also available canned and dried. In the southern USA, dried lima beans are often referred to as butter beans. The large European butter bean, or Madagascar bean, is a close relative to the lima bean and is most often available canned or dried. A traditional way to serve lima beans is combined with sweetcorn, molasses and paprika in the unusual native North American dish, *succotash*.

Broad bean

This flattish bean, also called the fava bean, resembles a very large lima bean and was the original staple of Europe, North Africa and the Middle East long before the introduction of the haricot bean from the Americas. Broad beans are available fresh, dried, canned or frozen. The pods of very young broad beans are edible and simply require 'topping and tailing'; they can be eaten raw. Old broad beans tend to have a very tough skin, which should be removed by blanching before cooking them.

They can be cooked in a variety of ways; falafel is a well-known Middle Eastern favourite, while in Europe broad beans are traditionally served stewed with ham or bacon.and herbs A small round variety of broad bean is the *ful medame*, used in the Egyptian national dish of the same name, in which the broad beans are baked with eggs and spices.

Butter bean

See Lima bean.

Haricot bean

Originally a native of Central America, the haricot bean (*Phaseolus vulgaris*) includes a large number of varieties – both climbing and bush species – widely grown in the USA, Europe and elsewhere. Varieties include certain green beans, kidney, pinto and borlotti beans and flageolets (*see individual entries*). Haricot bean seeds (as opposed to the pods) are sold either fresh after being dried in their pods.

In France and Britain, 'haricot bean' generally now refers to small, smooth, white, dried beans, which are oval rather than kidney-shaped. The best of these, the soisson, comes from France and is used in the classic dish, cassoulet.

pinto beans

aduki beans

black-eyed beans

mung beans

red lentils

green lentils

butter beans

flageolet beans

black beans

Varieties and Identification

In the USA such haricots are called white beans. Varieties include the navy (or Yankee) bean, used as a staple by the US navy since the mid-1800s, and the pea bean. Both are used to make Boston baked beans and for canning.

Kidney bean

The red kidney bean is a type of haricot bean – firm, with a dark red glossy skin and cream flesh. It is a staple in Central America and is used interchangeably with the pinto bean to make *frijoles refritos* (refried beans). Elsewhere, it is probably best known for its use in chilli con carne. It is more readily available dried or canned than fresh.

The black kidney bean, also called the turtle bean, has the same uses as the red kidney bean and the pinto bean and again features in many Central and South American dishes, notably the Brazilian national dish *feijoada*.

White kidney, or cannellini, beans are less flavoursome and are available only dried or canned. They are popular in Italian cooking, particularly in salads, casseroles and soups.

Pinto bean

A variety of haricot bean grown in Latin America and the southwest USA, this pale pink bean is streaked with reddish-brown. Pinto (Spanish for 'painted') beans are widely used in Tex-Mex cooking and Mexican bean dishes, especially *frijoles refritos*, and are often served with rice or used in soups and stews. The pinto bean can be used interchangeably with the pink bean, which is lighter in colour before cooking but looks the same afterwards. Pinto beans are available in dried form.

Borlotti bean

Another dried bean from the haricot family, this one is very popular in Italy. The bean is light brown or pink and speckled with deeper red. It resembles the pinto bean in appearance, and is typically used in Italian regional stews and soups.

Flageolet bean

Usually white or pale green, this tiny, tender French haricot bean has a creamy, delicate flavour. It is available fresh, dried, canned and sometimes frozen. It is most often served with lamb or ham.

Cannellini bean

See Kidney bean.

Black-eyed bean

This small whitish/beige bean with a distinctive spot of black at its inner curve is also called the black-eyed pea, cowpea and, if the 'eye' is yellow, yellow-eyed pea. The bean was introduced from Africa to Europe and America via slave traders in the late 17th century. It is generally sold dried although it is available fresh in the southern USA, where it is an essential ingredient in the dish hoppin' John, traditionally served on New Year's Day to bring good luck.

Soya bean (soybean, soy pea, soja, soi)

There are over a thousand varieties of soya bean, ranging in size and colour (white, yellow, green, red, brown and black). The soya bean has a high nutritive value and is used to produce a wide variety of products including tofu (soya bean curd), soya bean oil, soya flour, soya milk (useful for those allergic to dairy products), textured vegetable protein (TVP), fermented black beans and bean pastes, and sauces such as soy sauce, shoyu, miso, kecap and tamari. Soya beans can be soaked and cooked like any other dried beans for use in soups, stews and casseroles, although they are quite tough. They can also be sprouted to produce bean sprouts, and used in salads or as a cooked vegetable. Fresh soya beans are not generally available except in Asian or speciality produce markets.

Salted black bean

This is a small soya bean, which is fermented and salted. Salted black beans have a strong flavour and are used in Chinese cooking as a savoury seasoning. They are available dried or canned.

Aduki bean (asuki bean, adzuki bean)

This small, dried, dark red starchy bean is particularly popular in Japanese and Chinese cooking and can be purchased whole or powdered in Asian food stores. The bean's sweet flavour has led to its use in oriental confectionery, and its flour is used for making cakes and pastries.

Mung bean

A small cylindrical bean, most commonly olive-green in colour with a yellow interior but brown and black varieties exist. Widely used in Asian cooking, whole mung beans are a popular ingredient in soups, stews and pilafs. They are often used in Europe to produce bean sprouts.

Chickpea

Although not actually a bean, this small round, irregularly shaped, pale brown legume with its firm texture and mild, nutty flavour, is used in similar ways. Chickpeas (also called garbanzo beans, ceci and, in India, chana) are used extensively in the Mediterranean countries, India and the Middle East – in salads, soups and stews and in dishes such as hummus. Chickpeas can be ground to produce gram flour, or besan, which is used extensively in Indian cooking. Chickpeas are available canned and dried; dried chickpeas need lengthy soaking and simmering to become really tender and delicious.

Varieties and Identification

Lentils

Available both whole and split, dried lentils are popular in parts of Europe and are a staple throughout much of the Middle East and India. They require no soaking and disintegrate quite quickly on cooking. They can be used as a side dish (puréed or whole and combined with vegetables), in salads, soups and stews. Lentils are used in Indian cookery to make various spicy dhals ('dhal' in India is the general term for split pulses, as well as the dish made from them). The most familiar varieties of lentil include the small reddish-orange split lentil, originally from India; the large, flat, green-brown Continental lentil; and the very tiny, grey-green Puy lentil from France.

Baked beans

The canned baked beans in tomato sauce so familiar today are produced from US-grown navy and pea beans, which are varieties of haricot bean. The product's origins lie in a traditional New England dish called Boston baked beans. The original recipe involved baking navy beans or the smaller pea beans with salt pork, mustard, spices, molasses and brown sugar in a slow oven for hours until tender. It was traditionally made by Puritan Bostonian women to be eaten on Saturday night; the leftovers were served with heavy Boston brown bread on the Sabbath when cooking was forbidden. Canned baked beans are available with reduced or no added salt and sugar, and with extra ingredients such as pork sausages or bacon; organic baked beans are available, too. The popularity of canned baked beans has led to a whole range of more unusual products such as baked bean bolognaise, baked bean chilli con carne and baked bean pizza.

Like all beans, canned baked beans have good nutritive values. A 200 g (7 oz) serving of baked beans provides nearly half of the recommended daily fibre intake and more protein than an egg or 300 ml (½ pint) milk.

Choosing and storing

Fresh beans start to convert their sugar into starch from the moment they are picked. This process alters their taste and texture, so the fresher they are the better. Freshly picked peas or broad beans are infintely sweeter, crisper and more tender than those bought at the supermarket. Freezing halts the sugar-to-starch process so frozen beans are a good alternative to fresh.

Fresh beans

When buying any fresh beans, select ones that are crisp, brightly coloured and free of blemishes. A fresh green bean will snap rather than bend if it is fresh. Green beans can be stored in the refrigerator, in an air-tight container or tightly wrapped in a plastic bag, for up to 5 days. After this, their colour and flavour begin to diminish.

Avoid fresh broad beans whose pods are bulging with beans – this indicates age and mature beans are woolly and tasteless. Fresh broad beans can be kept in the refrigerator for 3–4 days; lima bean pods can be refrigerated in a plastic bag for up to a week.

Dried pulses

Shop for dried pulses where you know the turnover is brisk. Most varieties are available in supermarkets but those found in 'ethnic' stores or delicatessens selling their best national products, will probably be of better quality. Dried beans should be plump and brightly coloured with a soft sheen to their skin. Avoid any that are wrinkled, chipped or cracked, as these are probably quite old.

Dried pulses have a long shelf life and will keep well for up to a year if kept in a dry, airtight container at room temperature and away from the light. However, it is best to eat them as fresh as possible as they toughen with age and older ones will take longer to cook.

Preparing and Cooking

To prepare fresh green beans, cut off their tips (known as 'top and tail'), and remove any strings – a string will come away if you pull downwards as you remove the top or tail. Cut the beans thinly either diagonally across the pod or lengthways. Gently simmer, steam, microwave or stir-fry briefly until slightly crisp to the bite – take care not to overcook them. If the beans are to be served cold in a salad, plunging them into cold water immediately after cooking will help them retain their colour.

Cook lima beans briefly in boiling salted water. Similarly, young broad beans can be cooked in their pods in boiling salted water for 10–12 minutes until tender. Mature broad beans need shelling first before cooking for about 5 minutes. Drain the cooked mature beans then rinse under cold running water. Remove their whitish, rather tough outer skins to reveal the bright green, velvety bean inside.

Soaking dried pulses

Dried pulses are available prepackaged or in bulk. Many need to be soaked in water for several hours or overnight to rehydrate before cooking. Follow the packet or recipe instructions for best results. Dried beans labelled 'quick-cooking' have been presoaked and redried before packaging; they require no presoaking and so take less time to prepare. However, they are not as firm as ordinary dried beans.

In the past, dried pulses had to be picked over before use to extract small pieces of grit, tiny sticks and ungerminated seeds. This is rarely necessary nowadays. However, put them in a sieve and rinse thoroughly to remove any surface dust or dirt. Lentils, green and yellow split peas, black-eyed beans and mung beans are ready to be cooked once rinsed; other dried pulses require soaking first. Soaking times can be 4–12 hours, depending on the type and age of the pulse – soya beans and chickpeas are the hardest pulses and need soaking the longest. During the soaking process remove any immature or overdry specimens which won't cook properly, that float to the surface, and change the water two or three times to help counteract flatulence (*see page 9*).

There are two soaking methods: the conventional one involves putting the pulses in a large bowl, covering them with four times their volume of cold water and leaving them to stand. It is often convenient to soak pulses overnight – the longer they are allowed to soak, the softer they become and the quicker they cook. The alternative, quick-soak method involves putting the pulses in a saucepan with four times their volume of cold, unsalted water. Bring to the boil, then boil vigorously for 5 minutes. Cover the pan, remove from the heat and allow the pulses to stand for about 1 hour. Soaked

pulses are ready to cook when they are plump and fully swollen, with smooth skins. Dried pulses will roughly double in bulk during soaking. Left to soak in hot conditions, dried pulses may start to ferment and the soaking water will appear frothy. If this happens put the bowl in the refrigerator.

> **Beans safety**
> Boil soaked red kidney beans vigorously for 10 minutes at the start of cooking to destroy the toxins on their skins.

Cooking dried beans and chickpeas

Once the pulses have been soaked, drain – always discard the soaking water – and rinse them in fresh water. Place in a saucepan and cover with more fresh water until the water level is about 2.5–5 cm (1–2 inches) above the pulses. This is sufficient to prevent the pulses drying out; too much water allows more protein and carbohydrates to leach out of them, thus diminishing their nutritional value.

Bring the pulses to the boil then reduce the heat and simmer gently. The exception to this is red kidney beans, which must be boiled vigorously for 10 minutes before simmering to ensure that any toxins on the outside skins of the beans are completely destroyed. At one

Preparing and Cooking

time this 10-minute vigorous boiling was the accepted practice for all beans but it is not now considered necessary, although some cooks still advise it for aduki, black kidney and borlotti beans.

Continue simmering the beans gently until soft, frequently removing the scum that forms on the surface. Adding a little oil to the cooking liquid can help prevent the scum forming. The beans are cooked when soft to the bite and evenly coloured all the way through. The length of cooking time varies according to the type of pulse, the quantity of pulses being cooked and their age – old pulses can take twice as long to cook.

Seasonings such as garlic, onion, oregano, parsley or thyme can be added during cooking, but not acidic ingredients, such as tomatoes, vinegar, wine or lemon juice, which will increase the cooking time. It is better to add these ingredients only when the beans are almost tender. Similarly, while salt is necessary to bring out the flavour of dried beans, it can slow down the cooking and is best added towards the end when you can better gauge how much is required. At one time a pinch of bicarbonate of soda was added speed up cooking. This is not now recommended as it destroys nutrients. Take care not to overcook dried pulses since, with the exception of chickpeas, they will disintegrate and become mushy.

Cooked dried beans absorb other flavours well – even more so if the flavouring is added while the cooked beans are still hot. If the beans are required cold, leave to cool in their cooking liquid to prevent them drying out and their skins splitting.

Cooking lentils

To cook whole lentils, simply bring them to the boil in plenty of water (or stock or wine) and cook until just soft. To cook split lentils for a purée or pâté measure the water exactly according to the recipe, or the end result may be too sloppy.

> ### Canned pulses
> Canned pulses are already cooked and are a quick and convenient alternative to dried. Simply drain and rinse well to remove the canning liquid. To substitute canned beans for dried, remember that the weight of dried beans roughly doubles during soaking and cooking so a recipe that calls for 125 g (4 oz) dried beans would require about 250 g (8 oz) drained, canned beans. Check the labels of canned pulses for additives – many varieties will have had salt or sugar added.

Keeping cooked beans

Cooked dried beans keep well so it is worth cooking a large batch in one go and storing the excess in usable quantities. Plain boiled beans can be drained and stored in an airtight plastic container in the refrigerator for 5–6 days, beans cooked with onion will keep half that time. Alternatively, freeze cooked beans, either in their cooking liquid or drained, in airtight plastic containers for up to 6 months. Allow them to thaw overnight in the refrigerator, or for 2–3 hours at room temperature, or defrost them in a microwave. When reheating cooked beans, add 1–2 tablespoons of water.

Cooked bean dishes also keep well and can be kept refrigerated for 4–5 days.

Organic beans

Food that is certified and labelled 'organic' has been produced by strictly defined methods. Thus, organic beans have been grown without the use of artificial chemical fertilizers and pesticides, and they are free from any genetically modified organisms (GMOs). Organic processed foods such as canned baked beans contain no artificial flavourings or colourings.

Various types of organic beans are now available – in canned, dried and frozen form – for example canned cut green beans, butter beans, lentils, baked beans and chickpeas, and dried soya, black-eyed, butter, haricot, kidney and pinto beans. It is likely that many more bean varieties will become increasingly available in organic form.

Basic Recipes

Makes approx. 100 ml (3½ fl oz) / Preparation time: 3 minutes

Harissa

Harissa is a fiery red paste, a blend of red chillies, garlic and spices, widely used in North African cooking. It is used during the preparation of dishes and appears in small bowls on the table as a condiment. It is available commercially or you can make your own.

2 red peppers, roasted and skinned

25 g (1 oz) fresh red chillies, chopped, seeds
   retained

1–2 garlic cloves, crushed

½ teaspoon coriander seeds, toasted

2 teaspoons caraway seeds

olive oil

salt

1. Place the red peppers, the chillies and their seeds, garlic, coriander and caraway seeds and a pinch of salt in a blender or food processor. Blend the ingredients together, adding enough olive oil to make a thick paste.
2. Spoon the harissa into a small clean, dry jar and pour a layer of olive oil over the top to seal. Cover with a tight-fitting lid and store in the refrigerator.

Makes 10 lemons / Preparation time: 10 minutes

Preserved Lemons

10 lemons

coarse salt

1. Put 2 teaspoons coarse salt into a scalded Kilner jar. Holding one lemon over a plate to catch the juice, cut it lengthways as if about to quarter it, but do not cut quite through - leave the pieces joined. Ease out any pips. Pack 1 tablespoon salt into the cuts, then close them and place the lemon in the jar.
2. Repeat with the remaining lemons, packing them in tightly, and pressing each layer down hard before adding the next layer, until the jar is full. Squeeze another lemon and pour the juice over the fruit. Sprinkle with more coarse salt and top up with boiling water to cover the lemons. Close the jar tightly and keep in a warmish place for 3-4 weeks. Do not worry if, on longer storage, a lacy white film appears on top of the jar or on the lemons; it is quite harmless. Simply rinse it off.

Makes 1 litre (1¾ pints) / Preparation time: 5—10 minutes / Cooking time: about 45 minutes

Vegetable Stock

500 g (1 lb) chopped mixed vegetables, such as
   equal quantities of carrots, leeks, celery,
   onion and mushrooms

1 garlic clove

6 peppercorns

1 bouquet garni (2 parsley sprigs, 2 thyme sprigs
   and 1 bay leaf)

1.2 litres (2 pints) water

1. Place the chopped vegetables and garlic in a large saucepan and add the peppercorns and bouquet garni.
2. Cover with the water. Bring to the boil and simmer gently for 30 minutes, skimming off any scum when necessary. Strain and cool the stock completely before refrigerating.

Makes 1 litre (1¾ pints) / Preparation time: 5–10 minutes / Cooking time: about 45 minutes

Pesto

50 g (2 oz) basil leaves

1 garlic clove, crushed

2 tablespoons pine nuts

¼ teaspoon sea salt

6–8 tablespoons extra virgin olive oil

2 tablespoons freshly grated Parmesan cheese

pepper

1. Grind the basil, garlic, pine nuts and sea salt in a mortar or food processor to form a fairly smooth paste. Slowly add the oil until you reach the required texture, soft but not runny, and then add the cheese and pepper to taste. Transfer to a bowl and cover the surface with clingfilm.
2. Serve tossed with freshly cooked pasta, spooned on to soups or with grilled fish or chicken. Pesto can be kept chilled for up to 3 days in the refrigerator.

VARIATION
To make red pesto, add 25 g (1 oz) drained and chopped sun-dried tomatoes in oil to the basil and continue as above, omitting the Parmesan.

1

Soups and Starters

Serves: 8 very generously / Preparation time: 20 minutes, plus overnight soaking / Cooking time: about 3 hours

La Ribollita

This very filling bean and cabbage soup is one of Tuscany's most famous soups. La ribollita means 'reboiled' and refers to the fact that, traditionally, the soup was reheated and served day after day. To make it stretch further when there was little meat and vegetables to spare, bread was added. Even now, the soup is made the day before required then reheated. It is ladled over toasted garlic bread, drizzled with olive oil and served with plenty of Parmesan. Strictly speaking, the soup should be made with the delicious Tuscan black cabbage called cavolo nero, but Savoy cabbage is a good substitute.

75 ml (3 fl oz) extra virgin olive oil

1 onion, finely chopped

1 carrot, chopped

1 celery stick, chopped

2 leeks, trimmed, cleaned and finely chopped

4 garlic cloves, finely chopped

1 small white cabbage, shredded

1 large potato, chopped

4 courgettes, chopped

200 g (7 oz) dried cannellini beans, soaked
   overnight, drained and rinsed

400 ml (14 fl oz) passata

2 sprigs of rosemary

2 sprigs of thyme

2 sprigs of sage

1 dried red chilli

2.1 litres (3½ pints) water

500 g (1 lb) cavolo nero or Savoy cabbage,
   finely shredded

salt and pepper

To serve:

75 ml (3 fl oz) extra virgin olive oil, plus extra
   for drizzling

8 thick slices of crusty white country-style bread

1 garlic clove, bruised

freshly grated Parmesan cheese

1. Heat the oil in a heavy-bottomed saucepan. Add the onion, carrot and celery and cook gently for about 10 minutes, stirring frequently. Next add the leeks and garlic and cook for another 10 minutes. Add the white cabbage, potato and courgettes, stir well and cook for a further 10 minutes, stirring frequently.

2. Stir in the beans, passata, rosemary, thyme, sage, dried red chilli, salt and plenty of pepper. Cover with the water (the vegetables should be well covered) and bring to the boil, then reduce the heat and simmer, covered, for at least 2 hours, until the beans are very soft.

3. Remove 2–3 ladlefuls of soup, mash it well or purée in a blender or food processor then return to the soup. Stir in the cavolo nero or Savoy cabbage and simmer for another 15 minutes. Leave the soup to cool then refrigerate overnight.

4. The next day, slowly reheat the soup and stir in the olive oil. Toast the slices of bread and rub them with the bruised garlic. Arrange the bread over the base of a tureen or in individual bowls and ladle the soup over it. Drizzle with olive oil and serve with plenty of freshly grated Parmesan.

Butter Bean and Sun-dried Tomato Soup

Although it takes only a few minutes to prepare, this chunky soup distinctly resembles a robust Italian minestrone. It makes a worthy main course served with bread and plenty of Parmesan.

3 tablespoons extra virgin olive oil

1 onion, finely chopped

2 celery sticks, thinly sliced

2 garlic cloves, thinly sliced

2 x 425 g (14 oz) cans butter beans, drained
   and rinsed

4 tablespoons sun-dried tomato purée

900 ml (1½ pints) Vegetable Stock (see page 21)

1 tablespoon chopped rosemary or thyme

salt and pepper

Parmesan cheese shavings, to serve

1. Heat the oil in a saucepan. Add the onion and sauté for 3 minutes until softened. Add the celery and garlic and sauté for 2 minutes.

2. Add the butter beans, sun-dried tomato purée, vegetable stock, rosemary or thyme and a little salt and pepper. Bring to the boil, then reduce the heat, cover and simmer gently for 15 minutes. Serve sprinkled with Parmesan shavings.

Minestrone Soup

Minestrone actually improves in flavour when it is made in advance and reheated. Cover and store in the refrigerator so that the flavours can blend.

2 tablespoons extra virgin olive oil

1 onion, diced

1 garlic clove, crushed

2 celery sticks, chopped

1 leek, trimmed, cleaned and finely sliced

1 carrot, chopped

425 g (14 oz) can chopped tomatoes

600 ml (1 pint) chicken or Vegetable Stock
   (see page 21)

1 courgette, diced

½ small cabbage, shredded

1 bay leaf

75 g (3 oz) canned haricot beans, drained and
   rinsed

75 g (3 oz) dried spaghetti, broken into small
   pieces

1 tablespoon chopped flat leaf parsley

salt and pepper

To serve:

50 g (2 oz) Parmesan cheese, freshly grated

bruschetta

1. Heat the oil in a saucepan. Add the onion, garlic, celery, leek and carrot and sauté for 3 minutes.
2. Add the canned tomatoes, stock, courgette, cabbage, bay leaf and haricot beans. Bring to the boil and simmer for 10 minutes.
3. Add the broken spaghetti and season with salt and pepper to taste. Stir well and cook for a further 8 minutes. Keep stirring, as the soup may stick to the bottom of the pan.
4. Just before serving, add the chopped parsley and stir well. Serve with grated Parmesan and bruschetta.

FOOD FACT

Bruschetta comprises thick slices of country-style bread, toasted, rubbed with cut garlic and brushed with a well-flavoured olive oil. Italian breads such as focaccia or ciabatta or French *pain de campagne* or a baguette are suitable alternatives to serve with this chunky soup.

White Bean Soup with Garlic Sauce

More or less identical soups based on dried white beans are popular in Italy, particularly Tuscany, as well as in Greece and Turkey.

6 tablespoons extra virgin olive oil

2 garlic cloves, crushed

1 bay leaf

leaves from 2 sprigs of thyme and 2 sprigs
   of oregano

1 sage leaf, chopped

375 g (12 oz) dried cannellini beans or borlotti
   beans, soaked overnight, drained and rinsed

1.8 litres (3 pints) boiling water

1 large onion, chopped

2 carrots, chopped

1 head of celery, chopped

salt and pepper

finely chopped parsley, to garnish

Garlic sauce:

3 large egg yolks

4 tablespoons lemon juice

3 garlic cloves, crushed

175 g (6 oz) unsalted butter, melted until just
   bubbling

salt and pepper

1. Heat 4 tablespoons of the oil in a large heavy-bottomed saucepan. Add the garlic, herbs and beans and cook, stirring frequently, for about 5 minutes. Add the boiling water and simmer until the beans are tender – about 1 hour, depending on their age; add a little more water during cooking if necessary. Discard the bay leaf.

2. Meanwhile, heat the remaining oil in a frying pan, add the onion, carrots and celery, cover tightly and cook over a low heat, stirring occasionally, until soft – about 20 minutes.

3. Stir the vegetables into the beans and purée half the mixture in a blender or food processor. Return the purée to the remaining bean mixture in the pan, season and reheat gently.

4. To make the garlic sauce, mix the egg yolks, lemon juice, garlic and seasoning in a blender or food processor. With the motor running, slowly add the melted butter and continue mixing for a few minutes to make a thick, creamy sauce. Transfer to a warmed bowl.

5. To serve, pour the soup into warmed bowls. Add a spoonful of the sauce to each and sprinkle with finely chopped parsley.

Serves 6 / Preparation time: 20 minutes / Cooking time: 45 minutes

Mexican Soup with Avocado Salsa

A fiery soup that reflects the rich and contrasting flavours of Latin America, cooled by the subtle smoothness of an avocado salsa.

2 tablespoons sunflower oil

1 large onion, chopped

2 garlic cloves, crushed

2 teaspoons ground coriander

1 teaspoon ground cumin

1 red pepper, cored, deseeded and diced

3 red chillies, deseeded and sliced

425 g (14 oz) can red kidney beans, drained and rinsed

750 ml (1¼ pints) tomato juice

1–2 tablespoons chilli sauce

25 g (1 oz) tortilla chips, crushed

salt and pepper

sprigs of coriander, to garnish

Avocado salsa:

1 small ripe avocado

4 spring onions, finely chopped

1 tablespoon lemon juice

1 tablespoon chopped fresh coriander

salt and pepper

1. Heat the oil in a large, heavy-bottomed saucepan. Add the onion, garlic, spices, red pepper and two-thirds of the chillies, and fry gently for 10 minutes. Add the kidney beans, tomato juice and chilli sauce. Bring to the boil, cover and simmer gently for 30 minutes.

2. Meanwhile, make the avocado salsa. Peel, stone and finely dice the avocado. Place in a bowl and combine it with the spring onions, lemon juice and fresh coriander. Season with salt and pepper to taste, cover the bowl with clingfilm and set aside.

3. Purée the soup in a blender or food processor, together with the crushed tortilla chips. Return the soup to a clean saucepan, season to taste and heat through. Serve the soup at once with the avocado salsa, garnished with the reserved chilli slices and some sprigs of coriander.

Tasty Bean Soup

375 g (12 oz) dried haricot beans, soaked
    overnight, drained and rinsed

2.1 litres (3½ pints) water

1 carrot, chopped

1 onion, quartered

1 bouquet garni

125 g (4 oz) cooked smoked ham, cubed

40 g (1½ oz) butter

2 shallots, finely chopped

1 garlic clove, crushed

1 tablespoon chopped parsley, plus extra
    to garnish

olive oil, for drizzling

salt and pepper

croûtons, to serve

1. Place the beans in a large saucepan with the water and bring to the boil over a medium heat. Boil for 1½ hours, or until the beans are just tender.
2. Add the carrot, onion, bouquet garni and cubed ham and simmer for 20–30 minutes. Discard the bouquet garni then pour the soup into a blender or food processor. Purée until smooth, working in batches if necessary. Return the purée to the pan and reheat over a medium heat.
3. Meanwhile, melt the butter in a heavy-bottomed pan and gently fry the chopped shallots and garlic until golden but not browned. Add the chopped parsley and mix together quickly. Add half the shallot mixture to the bean purée.
4. Mix well with a wooden spoon, season with salt and pepper, then pour into warmed bowls. Sprinkle with croûtons, spooning the remaining shallot mixture on to them. Serve the soup hot, drizzled with olive oil and garnished with parsley.

Serves 6 / Preparation time: 15 minutes / Cooking time: about 50 minutes

Curried Green Bean Soup

50 g (2 oz) butter or margarine

1 garlic clove, crushed

1 onion, chopped

1 tablespoon mild curry powder

1.5 litres (2½ pints) Vegetable Stock
  (see page 21)

1 teaspoon chopped fresh marjoram or
  ½ teaspoon dried marjoram

1 bay leaf

500 g (1 lb) round green or French beans,
  trimmed and cut into 1 cm (½ inch) pieces

250–300 g (8–10 oz) potatoes, peeled
  and cubed

salt

150 ml (¼ pint) soured cream, to garnish

1. Melt the butter or margarine in a large saucepan and cook the garlic and onion over a moderate heat, until soft but not browned. Stir in the curry powder and cook for a further 2 minutes.

2. Pour in the vegetable stock. Add the marjoram, bay leaf, beans and potatoes, with salt to taste. Bring the mixture to the boil, then reduce the heat, cover the pan and simmer for 45 minutes, or until the vegetables are soft. Remove the bay leaf.

3. Purée the mixture in a blender or food processor, working in batches if necessary. Return the puréed soup to the pan. Stir well and heat gently, without boiling. Serve the soup in warmed bowls, each garnished with a swirl of soured cream.

Serves 4 / Preparation time: 10 minutes / Cooking time: 15 minutes

Black Bean Soup with Soba Noodles

200 g (7 oz) dried soba noodles

2 tablespoons groundnut or vegetable oil

1 bunch of spring onions, sliced

2 garlic cloves, roughly chopped

1 red chilli, deseeded and sliced

4 cm (1½ inch) piece of fresh root ginger, peeled and grated

125 ml (4 fl oz) black bean sauce or black bean stir-fry sauce

750 ml (1¼ pints) Vegetable Stock (see page 21)

200 g (7 oz) bok choy or spring greens, shredded

2 teaspoons soy sauce

1 teaspoon caster sugar

50 g (2 oz) raw, unsalted shelled peanuts

1. Cook the noodles in a saucepan of boiling water for about 5 minutes, or until just tender.

2. Meanwhile, heat the oil in a saucepan. Add the spring onions and garlic and sauté gently for 1 minute.

3. Add the red chilli, fresh ginger, black bean sauce and vegetable stock and bring to the boil. Stir in the bok choy or spring greens, soy sauce, caster sugar and peanuts; reduce the heat and simmer gently, uncovered, for 4 minutes.

4. Drain the noodles and pile into serving bowls. Ladle the soup over the noodles and serve immediately.

FOOD FACT

Soba noodles, traditional in Japanese cooking, are made from buckwheat and wholemeal flour, giving them a nutty flavour without the dryness of many wholemeal pastas.

Serves 4 / Preparation time: 3 minutes

Garlic, Herb and Bean Pâté

If you have only a few minutes to put together a snack or starter, this recipe is an ideal solution. Serve with some warm bread or crisp breads.

425 g (14 oz) can flageolet beans, drained and
    rinsed
125 g (4 oz) cream cheese
2 garlic cloves, chopped
3 tablespoons Pesto (see page 21)
2 spring onions, chopped
salt and pepper
chopped flat leaf parsley, to garnish (optional)

To serve:
25 g (1 oz) rocket leaves
16 radishes
8 crisp breads

1. Place the beans, cream cheese, garlic and pesto in a blender or food processor and process until combined.
2. Add the spring onions and salt and pepper and process for 10 seconds. Turn into a serving dish and chill until ready to serve. Serve with the rocket leaves and crisp breads, scattered with chopped parsley, if liked.

Bessara

250 g (8 oz) dried broad beans, soaked
   overnight, drained and rinsed
3 garlic cloves, crushed
1 teaspoon cumin seeds
extra virgin olive oil, for mixing and drizzling
salt

To serve:
za'atar (wild thyme) or mixed dried thyme,
   marjoram and oregano
warm bread
mixture of ground cumin, cayenne pepper
   and salt

This broad bean dip is as popular in North Africa as hummus is in the Middle East. The taste is similar, too. In Morocco, the dip is served with warm bread, which is first dipped into a mixture of ground spices before scooping up the purée.

1. Place the dried broad beans, garlic and cumin seeds in a saucepan. Add enough cold water to just cover and bring to the boil. Cover the saucepan and simmer for 1–2 hours – depending on the age and quality of the beans – until tender.
2. Drain the bean mixture, reserving the liquid. Rub the beans through a sieve, or purée them in a blender or food processor, adding enough of the reserved bean liquid and olive oil to make a cream. Season with salt to taste.
3. Serve the dip warm with extra oil trickled over the top and sprinkled with *za'atar* or a mixture of dried thyme, marjoram and oregano. Accompany with warm bread and a small bowl of mixed ground cumin, cayenne pepper and salt.

Serves 4–6 / Preparation time: 10 minutes, plus overnight soaking / Cooking time: 2½ hours

Refried Beans

This is a very popular dish in Central and South America, where it is known as *frijoles refritos*. The recipe involves frying beans that have been boiled and mashed.

250 g (8 oz) dried pinto beans, soaked
overnight, drained and rinsed
4 garlic cloves, crushed
1 bay leaf
4 tablespoons lard or bacon fat
175 g (6 oz) onion, chopped
salt and pepper
soured cream, to serve

To garnish:
sprigs of coriander
crushed mixed peppercorns

1. Place the beans in a large saucepan with the garlic and bay leaf. Cover with cold water and bring to the boil. Boil briskly for 10 minutes, then reduce the heat to a bare simmer and cook gently for about 2 hours, until the beans are very tender.
2. Drain the beans, reserving the cooking liquid. Discard the bay leaf. Mash the beans coarsely with a potato masher, or process in a blender or food processor, adding some of the reserved liquid as necessary until the desired consistency is achieved.
3. Melt the lard or bacon fat in a frying pan. Add the onion and sauté, stirring, until soft. Add the mashed beans and seasoning and mix well. Simmer until piping hot, continue to mash and add more liquid as necessary.
4. Serve the beans hot, topped with soured cream, garnished with coriander sprigs and crushed mixed peppercorns.

Chorizo with Broad Beans

Tapas bars serve this dish, or different versions of it, all over Spain. (See also page 41.)

250 g (8 oz) shelled young broad beans

1 tablespoon extra virgin olive oil

2 garlic cloves, roughly chopped

125 g (4 oz) spicy chorizo, cut into slices about
    5 mm (¼ inch) thick

1 tablespoon chopped dill

1 tablespoon chopped mint

2 tablespoons lemon juice

salt and pepper

crusty bread, to serve

1. Blanch the broad beans in a saucepan of lightly salted boiling water for 1 minute. Drain, rinse immediately under cold running water and drain again. Dry well.

2. Heat the oil in a frying pan, add the garlic and fry gently for 2–3 minutes until softened, then discard. Increase the heat, add the sliced chorizo and stir-fry for 2–3 minutes, until it is golden and has released some of its oil.

3. Stir in the blanched beans and cook for a further 2–3 minutes, then add the herbs and lemon juice and season to taste with salt and pepper. Mix well. Serve warm with crusty bread.

FOOD FACT

Chorizo is a cured or smoked Spanish salami-style sausage, made with coarsely chopped pork and flavoured with paprika, black pepper and garlic. Chorizo can be eaten raw or used as an ingredient in cooking.

Nut Koftas with Minted Yogurt

5–6 tablespoons groundnut oil or vegetable oil

1 onion, chopped

½ teaspoon dried chilli flakes

2 garlic cloves, roughly chopped

1 tablespoon medium curry paste

425 g (14 oz) can borlotti beans or cannellini beans, drained and rinsed

125 g (4 oz) ground almonds

75 g (3 oz) chopped honey-roast or salted almonds

1 small egg

200 g (7 oz) Greek yogurt

2 tablespoons chopped mint

1 tablespoon lemon juice

salt and pepper

warm naan bread, to serve

sprigs of mint, to garnish

1. Soak 8 bamboo skewers in hot water while preparing the koftas. Alternatively, use metal skewers, which do not require presoaking. Heat 3 tablespoons of the oil in a frying pan, add the onion and sauté for 4 minutes. Add the dried chilli flakes, garlic and curry paste and sauté for 1 minute.

2. Transfer to a blender or food processor with the beans, ground almonds, chopped almonds, egg and a little salt and pepper and process until the mixture starts to bind together.

3. Using lightly floured hands, take about one-eighth of the mixture and mould it around a skewer, forming it into a sausage shape, about 2.5 cm (1 inch) thick. Make 7 more koftas in the same way.

4. Place on a foil-lined grill pan and brush with 1 tablespoon of the remaining oil. Cook under a preheated moderate grill for about 5 minutes, until golden, turning once.

5. Meanwhile, mix together the yogurt and mint in a small serving bowl and season to taste with salt and pepper. In a separate bowl, mix together the remaining oil, the lemon juice and a little salt and pepper.

6. Brush the koftas with the lemon dressing and serve on warm naan bread, garnished with sprigs of mint. Serve the yogurt dressing separately.

Serves 4 / Preparation time: 10 minutes / Cooking time: 25 minutes

Broad Beans with Ham

Around the Mediterranean region there are innumerable variations on the theme of broad beans and ham or bacon. Some are more or less just the beans and ham; others have extra ingredients such as breadcrumbs and chopped hard-boiled egg, or carrots and potatoes. This Spanish version is colourful and tasty.

2 tablespoons extra virgin olive oil

4 large spring onions, finely chopped

1 red pepper, cored, deseeded and diced

50 g (2 oz) serrano ham, diced

500 g (1 lb) shelled broad beans

about 175 ml (6 fl oz) medium-bodied dry
   white wine

salt and pepper

1. Heat the oil in a saucepan. Add the spring onions, red pepper and ham and cook for 3 minutes.
2. Stir in the beans for 1 minute, then add sufficient wine to cover the vegetables. Bring quickly to the boil, cover the pan and simmer gently until the beans are tender, about 15–20 minutes. Uncover and boil off any excess liquid, if necessary. Add pepper and salt if necessary – this will depend on the saltiness of the ham. Cool slightly before serving.

VARIATION

Greek Broad Beans with Dill: Gently cook 2 bunches of sliced, plump spring onions in 3 tablespoons extra virgin olive oil in a heavy-bottomed pan, until soft. Stir in 625 g (1¼ lb) shelled fresh young broad beans and cook gently for 2–3 minutes. Add 2–3 tablespoons chopped dill, salt and pepper and sufficient water to just cover the beans. Cover and cook gently until the beans are tender. Serve with Greek ewes' milk yogurt.

Brown Beans and Egg with Lemon and Parsley Dressing

This dish makes a great starter or side salad. Health food stores and delicatessens are the most likely to stock brown beans. The canned variety tend to be large, flattish and quite bland, hence this spiced, tangy dressing. Canned red kidney beans or lima beans make a good substitute for brown beans.

425 g (14 oz) can brown beans, drained and
   rinsed
1 small pickled cucumber, roughly chopped
2 hard-boiled eggs, roughly chopped
salt and pepper
wholegrain bread, to serve

Dressing:

4 garlic cloves, crushed
1 teaspoon cumin seeds
½ bunch of spring onions, thinly sliced
small handful of parsley, chopped
1 tablespoon lemon juice
2 teaspoons Harissa (see page 20)
4 tablespoons extra virgin olive oil

1. To make the dressing, mix together the garlic, cumin seeds, spring onions, parsley, lemon juice, harissa and oil in a large bowl.
2. Mix the beans, cucumber and eggs together in another bowl, and season to taste with salt and pepper. Toss together gently, transfer to the bowl of dressing and mix thoroughly. Serve with wholegrain bread.

2 Vegetarian
Main Meals

Black Beans and Rice Cooked in Stout

1 teaspoon cumin seeds

1 teaspoon coriander seeds

3 tablespoons extra virgin olive oil

2 onions, chopped

3 garlic cloves, crushed

1 green chilli, deseeded and finely chopped

½ teaspoon chilli powder

2 teaspoons thyme leaves

500 g (1 lb) dried black kidney beans, soaked
   overnight, drained and rinsed

2 bay leaves

2 tablespoons black treacle

500 g (1 lb) tomatoes, skinned and chopped

300 ml (½ pint) stout

1 litre (1¾ pints) water

175 g (6 oz) long grain rice

4 tablespoons chopped fresh coriander

salt and pepper

Salsa:

4 spring onions, finely sliced

1 garlic clove, chopped

4 tomatoes, chopped

1 tablespoon chopped fresh coriander

75 g (3 oz) canned sweetcorn kernels, drained

2 tablespoons fresh lime juice

1. Place the cumin and coriander seeds in a frying pan and dry-fry over a moderate heat, stirring, for 1–2 minutes until fragrant – do not let them burn. Leave to cool, then grind to a powder in a spice grinder or using a pestle and mortar. Alternatively, put them into a small bowl and crush them with the end of a rolling pin. Set aside.

2. Heat the oil in a large flameproof casserole. Add the onions, garlic, green chilli, chilli powder and thyme and cook for 6–8 minutes until softened. Add the beans, the ground cumin and coriander seeds and the remaining ingredients, except the rice and fresh coriander.

3. Bring to the boil, then reduce the heat, cover and simmer over a very low heat for 1½–2 hours. Check occasionally and top up with boiling water if the mixture seems dry.

4. Add the rice and season with salt and pepper to taste. Cover and cook for a further 30 minutes, or until the beans and rice are very tender. Remove from the heat and stir in the chopped fresh coriander. Cover and leave for 5 minutes.

5. To prepare the salsa, mix all the ingredients together in a bowl. Serve the salsa as an accompaniment to the beans and rice.

Serves 4 / Preparation time: 15 minutes, plus overnight soaking / Cooking time: about 1 hour 20 minutes

Courgette and Bean Provençal

175 g (6 oz) dried cannellini beans, soaked
  overnight, drained and rinsed
3 tablespoons extra virgin olive oil
2 onions, sliced
2 garlic cloves, chopped
500 g (1 lb) courgettes, diced
425 g (14 oz) can chopped tomatoes
2 tablespoons tomato purée
2 teaspoons chopped oregano or thyme
1 bouquet garni
50 g (2 oz) black olives, halved and pitted
salt and pepper
sprigs of oregano and oregano leaves, to garnish

1. Place the beans in a large saucepan, cover with fresh water and bring to the boil. Cover and simmer for ¾–1 hour until almost tender, adding salt towards the end of the cooking time. Drain, reserving 150 ml (¼ pint) of the cooking liquid.
2. Meanwhile, heat the oil in a saucepan and fry the onions until soft but not browned. Add the garlic and courgettes and fry gently, stirring occasionally, for a further 15 minutes.
3. Add the tomatoes, tomato purée, oregano or thyme, bouquet garni, salt and pepper, the drained beans and reserved liquid. Cover and simmer for 20 minutes, adding the olives 5 minutes before the end of the cooking time. Serve immediately, garnished with oregano sprigs and leaves.

Braised Soya Beans with Shiitake Mushrooms and Spinach

This delightful combination of ingredients and flavours provides a tasty and nutritious dish. It is easy to prepare and makes an ideal mid-week supper dish.

175 g (6 oz) soya beans, soaked overnight, drained and rinsed

3 tablespoons extra virgin olive oil

1 garlic clove, chopped

1 teaspoon grated fresh root ginger

2 red chillies, deseeded and chopped

125 g (4 oz) shiitake mushrooms, sliced

4 ripe tomatoes, skinned, deseeded and chopped

2 tablespoons dark soy sauce

2 tablespoons dry sherry

250 g (8 oz) spinach leaves, washed and shredded

1. Place the beans in a saucepan with plenty of cold water. Bring to the boil and boil rapidly for 10 minutes, then reduce the heat, cover and simmer for 1 hour, or until the beans are tender. Drain, reserving 150 ml (¼ pint) of the cooking liquid.

2. Heat the oil in a large frying pan. Add the garlic, ginger and chillies and fry for 3 minutes. Add the mushrooms and fry for a further 5 minutes until tender.

3. Add the tomatoes, beans, reserved liquid, soy sauce and sherry and bring to the boil. Cover and simmer for 15 minutes.

4. Stir in the spinach and heat through for 2–3 minutes until the spinach has wilted. Serve at once.

**Serves 4–6 as a side dish, 4 as a supper dish / Preparation time: 10 minutes /
Cooking time: 10 minutes**

Mixed Bean Ratatouille

Served with a generous topping of freshly grated
Parmesan and with crusty French bread, this dish
makes a nutritious vegetarian supper. Ring the
changes with the ingredients if you like, using
different kinds of canned beans, or substituting
another fresh vegetable such as mangetout or
baby corn for the green beans.

175 g (6 oz) green beans, trimmed and halved
2 tablespoons vegetable oil
1 onion, finely chopped
2 garlic cloves, crushed
425 g (14 oz) can tomatoes
2 tablespoons tomato purée
1 teaspoon dried mixed herbs
¼–½ teaspoon sugar, according to taste
425 g (14 oz) can cannellini beans, drained and
  rinsed
2 tablespoons chopped basil, plus extra
  to garnish
salt and pepper

1. Blanch the halved green beans in a saucepan of lightly salted boiling water for
   2 minutes. Drain, rinse immediately under cold running water and drain again.
   Set aside.
2. Heat the oil in a saucepan. Add the onion and garlic and fry for 2–3 minutes, or
   until softened, but not browned.
3. Add the tomatoes, stir to mix with the onion and garlic and break them up with a
   wooden spoon. Add the tomato purée, dried mixed herbs, sugar and salt and
   pepper to taste. Bring to the boil, stirring constantly.
4. Add the green beans and canned beans to the saucepan. Toss until piping hot
   and coated in the tomato sauce. Remove from the heat and stir in the basil. Taste
   for seasoning and adjust if necessary. Serve at once, garnished with basil.

Serves 8 / Preparation time: 15 minutes, plus overnight soaking / Cooking time: 2¾ hours / Oven temperature: 150°C (300°F), Gas Mark 2

Bean Tagine

Tagine is the traditional name for both a North African cooking pot and the thick stew of meat and/or vegetables cooked slowly within it. An authentic everyday tagine is a shallow round earthenware pot with a tall conical lid.

500 g (1 lb) dried red or white kidney beans, soaked overnight, drained and rinsed

2 celery sticks, halved

2 bay leaves

4 sprigs of parsley

4 tablespoons extra virgin olive oil

500 g (1 lb) onions, chopped

5 garlic cloves, crushed

2 red chillies, deseeded and chopped

4 red peppers, cored, deseeded and chopped

1 tablespoon paprika

large handful of mixed chopped mint, parsley and coriander

salt and pepper

mint leaves, to garnish

Harissa (see page 20), to serve

Tomato sauce:

1 kg (2 lb) canned chopped tomatoes

2 tablespoons extra virgin olive oil

4 sprigs of parsley

1 tablespoon sugar

1. Boil the beans vigorously in a large saucepan of unsalted water for 10 minutes then drain. Tie the celery, bay leaves and parsley together with kitchen string. Cover the beans with fresh unsalted water, add the celery and herbs and simmer for about 1 hour until the beans are just tender. Drain, reserving the cooking liquid, and discard the celery and herbs.

2. Meanwhile, make the sauce. Empty the tomatoes and their juice into a saucepan, add the oil, parsley and sugar and bring to the boil then simmer, uncovered, for about 20 minutes until thick.

3. Heat the oil in a heavy-bottomed flameproof casserole. Add the onions, garlic, chillies, red peppers and paprika and cook gently for 5 minutes. Stir in the beans, the tomato sauce and enough of the reserved cooking liquid to just cover the beans. Season with salt and pepper, cover and cook in a preheated oven, 150°C (300°F), Gas Mark 2, for 1½ hours, stirring occasionally.

4. Just before serving, stir in the mint, parsley and coriander. Garnish with the mint leaves and serve with a bowl of harissa.

250 g (8 oz) dried lima or flageolet beans,
 soaked overnight, drained and rinsed

75 g (3 oz) butter

3 garlic cloves, crushed

2 shallots or 1 small onion, finely chopped

2 small fennel bulbs, finely sliced

1 red pepper, cored, deseeded and chopped

3 fresh sweetcorn cobs, husk and inner silks
 removed, cut into 2.5 cm (1 inch) rounds, or
 200 g (7 oz) canned or frozen sweetcorn
 kernels, defrosted if frozen

750 ml (1¼ pints) Vegetable Stock (see page 21)

2 tablespoons sherry or white wine vinegar

salt and pepper

Fennel and Corn Succotash

Succotash is a traditional native American vegetable stew. The key ingredients are lima beans and sweetcorn, although other beans – haricot, flageolet, black beans, black-eyed beans or a mixture of two or three varieties – can also be used. This version includes the aniseed flavour of fennel bulbs, which goes particularly well with the sweetcorn.

1. Place the beans in a large saucepan with sufficient water to cover. Bring to the boil, reduce the heat, cover and simmer for ¾–1 hour, or until tender. Drain and set aside.

2. Meanwhile, melt the butter in a large, heavy-bottomed saucepan. Add the garlic and shallots or onion and cook for 5 minutes until lightly browned. Add the fennel and red pepper and cook for 15–20 minutes until softened.

3. Add the sweetcorn, if using fresh, and the vegetable stock; season to taste. Bring to the boil, reduce the heat, cover and simmer for 20–30 minutes until the corn is tender. Remove the lid, add the drained beans, the canned or defrosted frozen corn, if using, and the vinegar.

4. Bring the succotash back to the boil and cook for about 5 minutes until the liquid has reduced and thickened slightly. Adjust the seasoning to taste and serve hot.

Breton Beans with Cheese and Herb Crust

3 tablespoons extra virgin olive oil

2 large onions, finely sliced

2–3 garlic cloves, chopped

2 large courgettes, cut into 1 cm (½ inch) dice

2 red peppers, cored, deseeded and diced

2 x 425 g (14 oz) cans chopped tomatoes

1 tablespoon double concentrate tomato purée

2 x 425 g (14 oz) cans butter or other white
    beans, drained and rinsed

150 ml (¼ pint) Vegetable Stock (see page 21)

1 tablespoon finely chopped parsley

2 bay leaves

1 teaspoon sugar

salt and pepper

mixed salad leaves, to serve (optional)

Cheese and herb crust:

1 small baguette, very thinly sliced

2 tablespoons extra virgin olive oil

2 tablespoons finely chopped basil

1 tablespoon finely chopped parsley

50 g (2 oz) Parmesan cheese, finely grated

1. Heat the oil in a large saucepan or flameproof casserole dish and fry the onions and garlic until soft but not browned. Add the courgettes and continue to fry for a few minutes until beginning to brown. Add all the remaining ingredients except salt and stir well to combine.

2. Bring to the boil, reduce the heat, cover and simmer until the tomatoes are thick and pulpy and the flavours blended – about 30–40 minutes. Taste and adjust the seasoning, adding salt if necessary.

3. Uncover the stew. To make the cheese and herb crust, brush the bread slices with oil, arrange on top of the stew and scatter with the herbs and Parmesan. Place the pan under a preheated grill and toast until the bread is golden brown and crisp. Serve immediately with mixed salad leaves, if liked.

Orzo Pilaf with Beans and Mint

This is a slightly unusual pilaf using orzo, a tiny rice-shaped pasta, sometimes called risi, and lots of fresh mint. Orzo is available from Italian delicatessens.

4 tablespoons extra virgin olive oil

1 onion, finely chopped

2 leeks, trimmed, cleaned and sliced

2 garlic cloves, crushed

½ teaspoon ground cumin

pinch of saffron threads

375 g (12 oz) orzo

2 sprigs of mint, plus 4 tablespoons
    chopped mint

300 ml (½ pint) Vegetable Stock (see page 21)

250 g (8 oz) French beans, trimmed

50 g (2 oz) pine nuts, toasted and chopped

25 g (1 oz) butter

salt and pepper

1. Heat the oil in a large frying pan and fry the onion, leeks, garlic, cumin and saffron for 10 minutes, until the vegetables are softened but not browned.

2. Add the orzo and stir-fry for 1 minute, until all the grains are glossy. Add the sprigs of mint and vegetable stock and bring to the boil. Cover and simmer for 15–20 minutes, until the orzo is cooked and most of the liquid has been absorbed.

3. Meanwhile, blanch the beans in a saucepan of lightly salted boiling water for 3–4 minutes until al dente. Drain well.

4. Stir the beans into the orzo with the pine nuts, chopped mint and butter, and season with salt and pepper. Cover and cook over a very low heat for 10 minutes. Remove from the heat but leave to stand for a further 10 minutes before serving.

**Serves 6–8 / Preparation time: 15 minutes /
Cooking time: 2 hours / Oven temperature: 180°C (350°F), Gas Mark 4**

Speedy Mixed Baked Beans

425 g (14 oz) can red kidney beans

425 g (14 oz) can haricot beans

425 g (14 oz) can aduki beans or mung beans

250 ml (8 fl oz) passata

2 tablespoons molasses

½ tablespoon wholegrain mustard

1 tablespoon vegetarian Worcestershire sauce or
   dark soy sauce

½ teaspoon salt

pinch of ground cloves

1 large onion, finely chopped

2 carrots, diced

2 celery sticks, chopped

2 bay leaves

4 tablespoons chopped parsley

To serve:

grated vegetarian Cheddar cheese, (optional)

crusty bread

You may look at the cooking time and decide 'speedy' is a slight exaggeration, but the traditional method for Boston baked beans (the precursor of today's canned baked beans in tomato sauce) takes 6 hours to cook, plus overnight soaking of the beans.

1. Strain the liquid from the canned beans and pour half into a bowl, discarding the rest. Whisk the passata, molasses, mustard, Worcestershire or soy sauce, salt and cloves into the liquid until evenly combined.
2. Place the beans and all the remaining ingredients except the parsley into a casserole and stir in the liquid. Cover with a tight-fitting lid.
3. Transfer to a preheated oven, 180°C (350°F), Gas Mark 4, and bake for 2 hours. Stir in the chopped parsley and serve in warmed bowls topped with the cheese, if using, and accompanied by crusty bread.

VARIATION

Crusted Beans: Combine 50 g (2 oz) fresh wholemeal breadcrumbs with 50 g (2 oz) grated vegetarian Cheddar and 25 g (1 oz) ground almonds. Sprinkle over the beans after 1½ hours and return to the oven, uncovered, for a further 30 minutes to crisp up the topping.

Penne with Broad Beans and Artichoke Pesto

375 g (12 oz) dried penne

375 g (12 oz) frozen broad beans

75 g (3 oz) marinated charred artichokes, roughly chopped

1 garlic clove, chopped

15 g (½ oz) parsley, chopped

1 tablespoon pine nuts

15 g (½ oz) pecorino cheese, grated, plus extra to serve

150 ml (¼ pint) extra virgin olive oil

salt and pepper

1. Cook the pasta in a large saucepan of lightly salted boiling water for 10–12 minutes, or according to packet instructions, until tender but still firm to the bite. At the same time, blanch the broad beans in a saucepan of lightly salted boiling water for 3 minutes. Drain and set aside.

2. Meanwhile, put the artichokes, garlic, parsley and pine nuts in a blender or food processor and process until fairly smooth. Transfer the mixture to a bowl and stir in the pecorino and oil and season to taste with salt and pepper.

3. Drain the pasta, reserving 4 tablespoons of the cooking liquid, and return it to the pan. Add the artichoke pesto mixture, the broad beans and the reserved cooking liquid and season to taste with pepper. Toss over a medium heat until warmed through. Serve with extra grated pecorino.

FOOD FACT

Marinated charred artichokes are often sold in jars. If you cannot find them, use canned artichoke hearts instead.

**Serves 4 / Preparation time: 10 minutes, plus overnight soaking /
Cooking time: 3¼–3¾ hours / Oven temperature: 150°C (300°F), Gas Mark 2**

Butter Beans in Tomato Sauce

250 g (8 oz) dried butter beans, soaked
   overnight, drained and rinsed
3 tablespoons extra virgin olive oil, plus extra
   to serve
1 small onion, finely chopped
2 garlic cloves, crushed
¼ teaspoon dried chilli flakes
200 g (7 oz) can chopped tomatoes
1 tablespoon tomato purée
1 tablespoon dried oregano, plus extra to serve
salt and pepper

1. Place the beans in a large saucepan and cover generously with cold water. Bring to the boil then simmer for 1¼–1½ hours, until they start to feel tender.
2. Drain the beans, reserving the cooking liquid. Place the beans in a casserole with the oil, onion, garlic, dried chilli flakes, tomatoes, tomato purée and oregano and season with salt and pepper.
3. Add enough of the reserved cooking liquid to cover the beans, then bake, covered, in a preheated oven, 150°C (300°F), Gas Mark 2, for 1½ hours. Remove the lid and cook for a further 30–45 minutes, until the liquid is reduced and thickened. Serve the beans drizzled with a little olive oil and sprinkled with some more dried oregano.

Cannellini Beans with Leeks and Rocket

The creaminess of the beans and their sauce is nicely balanced by the peppery
rocket, stirred in at the last minute until it has just wilted.

125 g (4 oz) dried cannellini beans, soaked
   overnight, drained and rinsed

1.2 litres (2 pints) water

2 tablespoons walnut oil

2 leeks, trimmed, cleaned and sliced

1 tablespoon mustard seeds

1 garlic clove, crushed

125 g (4 oz) French beans, trimmed and halved

75 ml (3 fl oz) double cream

125 g (4 oz) rocket

2 tablespoons snipped chives

salt and pepper

1. Place the beans in a saucepan with the water. Bring to the boil and boil rapidly for 10 minutes. Reduce the heat and simmer gently for 45–50 minutes until the beans are tender.

2. Strain the liquid from the beans into a pan and boil it rapidly until reduced to 300 ml (½ pint). Reserve.

3. Heat the oil in a saucepan and fry the leeks, mustard seeds and garlic for 5 minutes. Add the drained beans, French beans and reduced stock and simmer gently for 5 minutes until the French beans are tender. Remove from the heat. Strain the liquid into a small saucepan, add the cream and boil for 2–3 minutes until slightly reduced.

4. Stir the rocket and chives into the beans and drizzle the sauce over. Season to taste and serve at once.

Broad Bean, Lemon and Parmesan Risotto

1 tablespoon butter

2 tablespoons extra virgin olive oil

1 onion, chopped

2 garlic cloves, crushed

400 g (13 oz) risotto rice

150 ml (¼ pint) dry white wine

1.2 litres (2 pints) hot Vegetable Stock
    (see page 21)

150 g (5 oz) fresh or frozen broad beans

50 g (2 oz) Parmesan cheese, grated, plus extra
    to serve

finely grated rind and juice of 1 lemon

salt and pepper

thyme leaves, to garnish

FOOD FACT

Risotto rice absorbs a large quantity of liquid during cooking. The grains of rice swell; they remain separate yet stick together to make a creamy risotto in which the rice is soft but firm, not sticky or mushy. Arborio, Vialone Nano and Carnaroli are the three Italian varieties suitable for risotto making.

1. Melt the butter with the oil in a large, heavy-bottomed saucepan. Add the onion and garlic and sauté gently for 3 minutes. Add the rice and cook for 1 minute, stirring.

2. Add the wine and cook, stirring, until the wine has been absorbed. Add a little stock and cook, stirring, until almost absorbed. Continue in the same way, gradually adding more stock, until half the stock is used. Stir in the beans.

3. Gradually add the remaining stock, a little at a time, until the mixture is thickened and creamy but still retaining a little bite. This will take 15–18 minutes. Stir in the Parmesan, lemon rind and juice, and season to taste with salt and pepper. Turn on to warmed serving plates, sprinkle with thyme and serve with extra Parmesan.

Serves 4 / Preparation time: 10 minutes / Cooking time: 25 minutes

Black Bean and Cabbage Stew

4 tablespoons extra virgin olive oil

1 large onion, chopped

1 leek, trimmed, cleaned and chopped

3 garlic cloves, sliced

1 tablespoon paprika

2 tablespoons chopped marjoram or thyme

625 g (1¼ lb) potatoes, cut into small chunks

425 g (14 oz) can black beans or black-eyed
    beans, drained and rinsed

1 litre (1¾ pints) Vegetable Stock (see page 21)

175 g (6 oz) cabbage or spring greens, shredded

salt and pepper

crusty bread, to serve

1. Heat the oil in a large saucepan. Add the onion and leek and sauté gently for 3 minutes. Add the garlic and paprika and sauté for 2 minutes.
2. Add the marjoram or thyme, potatoes, beans and vegetable stock and bring to the boil. Reduce the heat, cover and simmer gently for about 10 minutes until the potatoes have softened.
3. Add the cabbage or spring greens and season to taste with salt and pepper. Simmer for 5 minutes longer and serve with crusty bread.

Red Beans with Coconut and Cashew Nuts

3 tablespoons groundnut or vegetable oil

2 onions, chopped

2 small carrots, thinly sliced

3 garlic cloves, crushed

1 red pepper, cored, deseeded and chopped

2 bay leaves

1 tablespoon paprika

3 tablespoons tomato purée

400 ml (14 fl oz) can coconut milk

200 g (7 oz) can chopped tomatoes

150 ml (¼ pint) Vegetable Stock (see page 21)

425 g (14 oz) can red kidney beans, drained
and rinsed

100 g (3½ oz) unsalted, shelled cashew nuts,
toasted

small handful of fresh coriander, roughly
chopped

salt and pepper

boiled black or white rice, to serve

1. Heat the oil in a large saucepan. Add the onions and carrots and sauté for 3 minutes. Add the garlic, red pepper and bay leaves and sauté for 5 minutes, or until the vegetables are soft and well browned.

2. Stir in the paprika, tomato purée, coconut milk, tomatoes, vegetable stock and beans and bring to the boil. Reduce the heat and simmer, uncovered, for 12 minutes, or until the vegetables are tender.

3. Stir in the cashew nuts and coriander, season to taste with salt and pepper and heat through for 2 minutes. Serve with boiled rice.

Cannellini Beans on Toast

This is another delicious quick and easy version of Boston baked beans, on which the commercial variety is based. Slightly spicy and sweet, it is comfort food at its best.

2 tablespoons groundnut or vegetable oil

1 onion, chopped

1 celery stick, thinly sliced

1 teaspoon cornflour

2 tablespoons water

425 g (14 oz) can cannellini beans, drained and rinsed

200 g (7 oz) canned chopped tomatoes

300 ml (½ pint) Vegetable Stock (see page 21)

1 tablespoon coarse grain mustard

1 tablespoon black treacle

1 tablespoon tomato ketchup

1 tablespoon vegetarian Worcestershire sauce

salt and pepper

toasted chunky bread, to serve

1. Heat the oil in a saucepan. Add the onion and celery and sauté for 5 minutes until golden. Blend the cornflour with the water and add to the pan with all the remaining ingredients.
2. Bring to the boil, reduce the heat slightly and cook, uncovered, for about 20 minutes, stirring frequently, until the mixture is thickened and pulpy. Pile on toast to serve.

Red Pepper and Bean Cakes with Lemon Mayonnaise

Pack these crisp bean cakes into warm pitta bread and serve with salad for a fairly substantial lunch or supper dish. Any unbaked bean cakes will keep in the refrigerator, covered with waxed paper, for a day or so.

75 g (3 oz) French beans, trimmed and roughly chopped

2 tablespoons groundnut or vegetable oil

1 red pepper, cored, deseeded and diced

4 garlic cloves, crushed

2 teaspoons mild chilli powder

425 g (14 oz) can red kidney beans, drained and rinsed

75 g (3 oz) fresh white breadcrumbs

1 egg yolk

oil, for shallow-frying

salt and pepper

Lemon mayonnaise:

4 tablespoons mayonnaise

finely grated rind of 1 lemon

1 teaspoon lemon juice

salt and pepper

1. Blanch the French beans in a saucepan of lightly salted boiling water for 1–2 minutes until softened. Drain.
2. Meanwhile, heat the oil in a frying pan and sauté the pepper, garlic and chilli powder for 2 minutes.
3. Transfer the mixture to a blender or food processor and add the red kidney beans, breadcrumbs and egg yolk. Process very briefly until the ingredients are coarsely chopped. Add the drained beans, season to taste with salt and pepper and process until the ingredients are just combined.
4. Turn the mixture into a bowl and divide into 8 portions. Using lightly floured hands, shape the portions into little 'cakes'.
5. Mix the mayonnaise with the lemon rind and juice, and season to taste with salt and pepper.
6. Heat the oil for frying in a large frying pan and pan-fry the cakes for about 3 minutes on each side until crisp and golden. Serve with the lemon mayonnaise.

Bean and Beer Casserole with Baby Dumplings

4 tablespoons groundnut or vegetable oil

1 onion, sliced

1 celery stick, sliced

1 parsnip, sliced

425 g (14 oz) can mixed beans, drained
   and rinsed

425 g (14 oz) can baked beans in tomato sauce

250 ml (8 fl oz) Guinness or stout

250 ml (8 fl oz) Vegetable Stock (see page 21)

4 tablespoons roughly chopped herbs (such as
   rosemary, marjoram, thyme)

150 g (5 oz) self-raising flour

75 g (3 oz) vegetable suet

2 tablespoons coarse grain mustard

8–9 tablespoons cold water

salt and pepper

1. Heat the oil in a large saucepan or flameproof casserole. Add the onion, celery and parsnip and sauté for 3 minutes. Add the mixed beans, baked beans, beer, vegetable stock and 3 tablespoons of the herbs. Bring to the boil and let the mixture bubble, uncovered, for 8–10 minutes, or until slightly thickened.

2. Meanwhile, mix the flour, suet, mustard, remaining herbs and a little salt and pepper in a bowl with enough of the cold water to make a soft dough.

3. Evenly distribute 8 spoonfuls of the dough in the saucepan or casserole and cover with a lid. Cook for 10 minutes more, or until the dumplings are light and fluffy. Serve immediately.

Black Bean Chilli

250 g (8 oz) dried black kidney beans, soaked
  overnight, drained and rinsed

1.5 litres (2½ pints) water

4 tablespoons extra virgin olive oil

250 g (8 oz) small mushrooms, halved

1 large onion, chopped

2 garlic cloves, crushed

2 large potatoes, cubed

1 red or green pepper, cored, deseeded
  and diced

2 teaspoons ground coriander

1 teaspoon ground cumin

2 teaspoons hot chilli powder

450 ml (¾ pint) passata

1 tablespoon fresh lime juice

25 g (1 oz) dark chocolate, chopped

2 tablespoons chopped fresh coriander

Avocado salsa:

1 small ripe avocado

4 spring onions, chopped finely

1 tablespoon lemon juice

1 tablespoon chopped coriander

salt and pepper

1. Place the beans in a saucepan with the water. Bring to the boil then boil rapidly for 10 minutes. Reduce the heat, cover and simmer for 45 minutes.

2. Heat half the oil in a large pan and stir-fry the mushrooms for 5 minutes. Remove from the pan and set aside. Add the remaining oil to the pan with the onion, garlic, potatoes, pepper and spices. Fry over a medium heat for 10 minutes.

3. Drain the beans, reserving the cooking liquid. Boil the liquid until reduced to 450 ml (¾ pint). Stir the beans into the pan containing the vegetables; add the reduced bean liquid, passata and mushrooms. Bring to the boil, cover and simmer for 30 minutes.

4. Meanwhile, make the avocado salsa. Peel, stone and finely dice the avocado and combine with the remaining ingredients, seasoning to taste. Cover and set aside.

5. Stir the lime juice, chocolate and fresh coriander into the chilli and cook for a further 5 minutes. Serve piping hot topped with a spoonful of the avocado salsa.

FOOD FACT

Passata is made from sieved, crushed tomatoes. It is available from good supermarkets in cartons, jars and bottles.

3

Main Meals

Serves 4 / Preparation time: 15 minutes / Cooking time: about 1 hour 10 minutes / Oven temperature: 180°C (350°F), Gas Mark 4

Baked Bean Cassoulet

4 tablespoons olive oil

4 chicken thighs or drumsticks, skinned

500 g (1 lb) herb sausages

50 g (2 oz) chorizo or pepperoni sausage, thinly sliced

2 onions, thinly sliced

150 ml (¼ pint) chicken stock

3 garlic cloves, crushed

several sprigs of thyme

2 x 425 g (14 oz) cans baked beans in tomato sauce

2 tablespoons Worcestershire sauce

2 tablespoons tomato purée

½ teaspoon ground cloves

75 g (3 oz) breadcrumbs

salt and pepper

1. Heat the oil in a large frying pan and fry the chicken pieces and sausages for about 10 minutes until golden. Add the chorizo or pepperoni and onions and fry for a further 2 minutes. Transfer to a casserole dish and add the stock, garlic and thyme. Cover and bake in a preheated oven, 180°C (350°F), Gas Mark 4, for 30 minutes.

2. Remove from the oven and stir in the baked beans, Worcestershire sauce, tomato purée, cloves and seasoning until evenly combined.

3. Sprinkle with the breadcrumbs and return to the oven, uncovered, for 25–30 minutes until the breadcrumbs are golden and the chicken is cooked. Serve hot.

Farmer-style Cannellini Beans

500 g (1 lb) dried cannellini beans, soaked
    overnight, drained and rinsed

2.1 litres (3½ pints) water

1 celery stick, chopped

2 bay leaves

125 g (4 oz) piece smoked bacon

50 g (2 oz) bacon fat

3 tablespoons extra virgin olive oil

½ onion, finely chopped

1 tablespoon chopped sage leaves

1 sprig of rosemary, plus extra to garnish

1 garlic clove, crushed

3 ripe plum tomatoes, skinned, deseeded
    and chopped

½ vegetable stock cube

2 tablespoons red wine

salt and pepper

1. Place the beans, water, celery and bay leaves in a large saucepan. Bring to the boil and simmer for at least 2 hours until tender. Drain.

2. Meanwhile, place the bacon in a small saucepan with sufficient water to cover it and boil for 10 minutes. Remove with a slotted spoon and cut into bite-sized pieces.

3. Chop the bacon fat and place in a large shallow pan with the oil. Add the onion, herbs and garlic; cook over a medium heat until the onion is golden.

4. Add the drained cooked beans, mix together, season with salt and pepper to taste and leave for 10 minutes to allow the flavours to mingle.

5. Add the tomatoes and boiled bacon to the beans. Crumble in the stock cube and stir in the red wine.

6. Leave the sauce to thicken a little, then taste and adjust the seasoning, if necessary. Serve hot, garnished with rosemary sprigs.

Fusilli with Broad Beans, Parma Ham and Mint

You can use any variety of dried pasta for this dish. Skinning the shelled beans is slightly laborious, but well worth the effort.

500 g (1 lb) shelled broad beans

375 g (12 oz) dried fusilli or other pasta shapes

4 tablespoons extra virgin olive oil

2 garlic cloves, finely chopped

150 ml (¼ pint) dry white wine

200 ml (7 fl oz) single cream

2 tablespoons chopped mint

4 slices of Parma ham, cut into thin strips

25 g (1 oz) Pecorino Sardo or Parmesan cheese, freshly grated, plus extra to serve

pepper

1. Blanch the beans in a large saucepan of lightly salted boiling water for 1 minute. Drain, rinse immediately under cold running water and drain again. Carefully peel away and discard the rather tough outer skins of the beans to reveal the bright green, velvety bean inside.
2. Cook the pasta in a large saucepan of lightly salted boiling water according to packet instructions, until al dente.
3. Meanwhile, heat the oil in a deep frying pan and gently fry the garlic until softened, but not browned. Add the wine and boil rapidly until it is reduced to about 2 tablespoons; then stir in the cream, mint and season with pepper and heat through.
4. Drain the pasta and add to the sauce with the beans, the Parma ham and Pecorino Sardo or Parmesan. Stir over the heat for about 30 seconds and serve with extra cheese.

Tagliatelle with Borlotti Beans

3 tablespoons extra virgin olive oil

75 g (3 oz) smoked bacon, cubed

1 onion, finely chopped

5 sage leaves

200 g (7 oz) canned borlotti beans, drained and
   rinsed

¼ tablespoon plain flour

1 tablespoon tomato purée

2 tablespoons hot chicken stock

2 tablespoons red wine

400 g (13 oz) dried or fresh tagliatelle

2 tablespoons grated Parmesan cheese

1 tablespoon grated pecorino cheese

salt and pepper

4 sprigs of sage, to garnish

1. Heat the oil in a large heavy-bottomed pan; add the bacon, onion and whole sage leaves. Cook over a medium heat until golden. Add the beans.

2. Mix the flour and tomato purée in a small bowl, then stir in the stock and wine. Pour into the bean mixture, stir with a wooden spoon and simmer over a low heat until the sauce thickens.

3. Meanwhile, cook the pasta in a large saucepan of lightly salted boiling water according to packet instructions, until al dente.

4. Remove the sage leaves from the sauce and discard. Taste the sauce and adjust the seasoning, if necessary. Drain the pasta, mix with the sauce and tip into a large, warmed serving dish. Add the Parmesan and pecorino and serve hot, garnished with sprigs of sage.

FOOD FACT

Pecorino is a hard round cheese made from
ewes' milk, used in a similar way to Parmesan.
Pecorino Sardo (from Sardinia) and Pecorino
Romano (from the area around Rome) are the
best known varieties.

Serves 4 / Preparation time: 15 minutes, plus overnight soaking / Cooking time: 1¾–2 hours

Italian Sausages and Beans with Sage

The Italian name for this dish is *salsiccie con fagioli all'uccelletto*. *Uccelletto* is Italian for a small bird such as a thrush or lark, and the Tuscan term *all'uccelletto* is used to describe this bean dish because it is flavoured with sage, a herb often used when cooking small birds.

250 g (8 oz) dried cannellini beans, soaked
    overnight, drained and rinsed

5 tablespoons extra virgin olive oil

500 g (1 lb) fresh Italian pork sausages,
    chopped

250 ml (8 fl oz) passata

2 garlic cloves, crushed

1 sprig of fresh sage or 2 teaspoons dried sage

salt and pepper

sage leaves, to garnish

1. Place the beans in a large saucepan, cover with fresh cold water and bring to the boil. Boil rapidly for 10 minutes, then reduce the heat and half cover with a lid. Simmer for 1¼ hours, or until the beans are tender, skimming off the scum and adding more water as necessary.
2. Drain the beans and reserve the cooking liquid.
3. Heat 3 tablespoons of the oil in a flameproof casserole or heavy-bottomed saucepan. Add the sausages and cook over a medium heat until browned on all sides. Add the passata, garlic, sage and salt and pepper to taste, and stir well to mix. Bring to the boil, then add the beans and a few spoonfuls of the cooking liquid. Cover and simmer, stirring frequently, for 15 minutes – the consistency should be quite thick. Adjust the seasoning to taste.
4. Just before serving, drizzle the remaining olive oil over the dish and garnish with sage leaves.

FOOD FACT

There are many different types of Italian fresh pork sausages (*salsiccie puro suino*). They can vary from mild to herby or spicy-hot in flavour; most have a high meat content. Visit an Italian delicatessen for the best choice. *Salsiccie a metro* is a long thin sausage, traditionally sold by the metre, although now more often sold by weight. *Luganega*, a variety of *salsiccie a metro*, and *salamelle*, which is sold in links, are both suitable for this recipe.

Serves 4–6 / Preparation time: 15 minutes, plus overnight soaking / Cooking time: 3½–4½ hours / Oven temperature: 150°C (300°F), Gas Mark 2

Campfire Bean Pot

500 g (1 lb) dried haricot beans, soaked overnight
25 g (1 oz) soft brown sugar
¼ teaspoon ground cinnamon
2 teaspoons mustard powder
4 tablespoons molasses or black treacle
1 large onion, chopped
2 garlic cloves, crushed
4 tomatoes, skinned and chopped
1 sprig of thyme
1 bay leaf
2 whole cloves
375 g (12 oz) piece rindless streaky bacon
50–75 ml (2–3 fl oz) dark rum (optional)
salt and pepper

To serve:
corn on the cob
sausages

1. Drain the beans, rinse well and place in a large flameproof casserole. In a small bowl, mix together the sugar, cinnamon, mustard and molasses or treacle, then add to the beans. Add the remaining ingredients, except the rum, pushing the bacon down into the centre of the beans.

2. Pour over water to cover, about 600 ml (1 pint), bring to the boil, cover the casserole with a tight-fitting lid and place in a preheated oven, 150°C (300°F), Gas Mark 2, for 3–4 hours. Check occasionally and top up with boiling water if it seems too dry.

3. Stir in the rum, if using, and adjust the seasoning to taste. Remove the bacon, slice it and place the slices on top of the casserole. Return to the oven and cook uncovered for 20–30 minutes. Serve with corn on the cob and sausages.

**Serves 4 / Preparation time: 15 minutes, plus marinating / Cooking time: 1¾ hours /
Oven temperature: 180°C (350°F), Gas Mark 4**

2 tablespoons salted black beans

1.5 kg (3 lb) roasting chicken

1 tablespoon vegetable oil

1 teaspoon dark sesame oil

6 spring onions, diagonally sliced

1–2 red chillies, deseeded and thinly sliced

3 tablespoons dry sherry

1 teaspoon sugar

1 tablespoon cornflour

3 tablespoons water

Marinade:

25 g (1 oz) fresh root ginger, peeled and
   coarsely grated

1–2 tablespoons soy sauce

pepper

To garnish:

spring onion fans (see Tip)

strips of red pepper

Chinese Chicken with Black Beans

1. Soak the salted black beans in cold water for 20 minutes; drain well and set aside.
2. Meanwhile, mix the marinade ingredients together, with pepper to taste, and use to coat the chicken inside and out. Place the chicken in a roasting bag, tie loosely and place in a roasting tin. Leave to marinate for 4–6 hours, then make several holes in the bag, following the manufacturer's instructions.
3. Cook the chicken in a preheated oven, 180°C (350°F), Gas Mark 4, for 1¼ hours. Remove the chicken from the bag, reserving the juices, and place it in the roasting tin. Increase the oven temperature to 200°C (400°F), Gas Mark 6, and cook for a further 25–30 minutes, until the juices run clear.
4. Meanwhile, heat the vegetable and sesame oils in a pan, add the spring onions and stir-fry over a high heat for 30 seconds. Add the chillies and drained black beans and cook for 2 minutes. Skim off as much fat as possible from the reserved contents of the roasting bag, add the remaining liquid to the pan with the sherry and sugar. Blend the cornflour with the water and stir into the mixture; cook until clear and syrupy.
5. Carve the chicken and arrange on a warmed serving dish. Pour over the black bean sauce. Garnish with spring onion fans and red pepper strips.

TIP

To make spring onion fans, trim the tops off the spring onions and remove the root base. Carefully slit both ends of each onion lengthways, leaving the middle section of the onion intact. Leave in a bowl of iced water until the spring onions have opened up into 'fan' shapes.

Serves 4–6 / Preparation time: 30 minutes, plus overnight soaking / Cooking time: 2½ hours / Oven temperature: 160°C (325°F), Gas Mark 3

Lamb, Haricot Bean and Chicory Casserole with a Breadcrumb Topping

250 g (8 oz) dried haricot beans, soaked
   overnight, drained and rinsed

2 tablespoons extra virgin olive oil

2 kg (4 lb) boneless leg or shoulder of lamb,
   trimmed and cut into 3.5 cm (1½ inch) cubes

1 large red or white onion, sliced

2 whole garlic cloves

400 g (13 oz) ripe tomatoes, skinned and chopped

2 tablespoons tomato purée

1 sprig of rosemary

3 red or white chicory heads, sliced into 1 cm
   (½ inch) strips, core removed

salt and pepper

parsley, to garnish

Breadcrumb topping:

125 g (4 oz) fresh white breadcrumbs

3 tablespoons extra virgin olive oil

2 tablespoons chopped flat leaf parsley

2 tablespoons finely grated Parmesan cheese

salt and pepper

1. Place the haricot beans in a saucepan with sufficient water to cover. Bring to the boil, reduce the heat and simmer for 30 minutes; drain.

2. Meanwhile, heat the olive oil in a large flameproof casserole over a moderate heat. Add the lamb, in batches, and brown well all over. Remove the browned meat with a slotted spoon and set aside.

3. Reduce the heat under the casserole, add the onion and garlic and cook gently for 8–10 minutes until softened. Add the tomatoes, tomato purée and rosemary together with the reserved meat and the cooked beans, and add sufficient water to cover – about 600 ml (1 pint). Bring to the boil, season, cover with a tight-fitting lid and place in a preheated oven, 160°C (325°F), Gas Mark 3, for 1½ hours.

4. Mix the topping ingredients together and season with salt and pepper. Remove the lid from the casserole, taste and adjust the seasoning, then sprinkle over the sliced chicory and the breadcrumb topping. Return the casserole to the oven for 20–30 minutes until the meat is tender and the topping is golden. Serve immediately, garnished with parsley.

Serves 6–8 / Preparation time: 20 minutes / Cooking time: 2–2½ hours

Lamb, Artichoke and Broad Bean Tagine

FOOD FACT

Artichokes in oil (which are now sold by many supermarkets) have a much better flavour and texture than canned artichokes. The oil left from the artichokes can be used in cooking, for tossing with pasta, rice or pulses and making salad dressings. If you can't get artichokes in oil, canned artichokes can be substituted but be sure to rinse them after draining.

pinch of saffron threads

2 tablespoons hot water

1 bunch of parsley

1 bunch of coriander

3 tablespoons olive oil or oil from the artichokes
  (see Food Fact)

1.5 kg (3 lb) leg or shoulder of lamb, cut into
  large chunks

1 onion, sliced

2 garlic cloves, crushed

250 ml (8 fl oz) stock or water

1 teaspoon ground coriander

1 teaspoon ground ginger

500 g (1 lb) jar artichokes in oil, drained

500 g (1 lb) frozen broad beans, thawed

2 Preserved Lemons (see page 20), rinds
  only, diced

pepper

coriander sprigs, to garnish

durum wheat grains (blé) or couscous, to serve

1. Soak the saffron in the hot water. Tie the bunches of parsley and coriander together with kitchen string.

2. Heat the oil in a flameproof casserole. Add the lamb in batches and fry until evenly browned. Transfer to kitchen paper to drain.

3. Stir the onion into the casserole and cook until softened and lightly browned, adding the garlic when the onion is almost ready. Return the meat to the casserole then pour in the stock or water and add the coriander, ginger, saffron and herbs. Cover the casserole tightly and cook gently, stirring occasionally, for about 1¼ hours or until the lamb is just tender.

4. Stir the artichokes, broad beans and preserved lemon rinds into the casserole, cover and cook for a further 30 minutes. To serve, discard the bunches of herbs, season to taste and garnish with coriander. Serve with wheat or couscous.

Serves 4–6 / Preparation time: 30 minutes, plus overnight soaking / Cooking time: 2½–3 hours / Oven temperature: 160°C (325°F), Gas Mark 3

New Mexican Beef and Bean Stew with Corn Dumplings

375 g (12 oz) dried red or black kidney beans, soaked overnight, drained and rinsed

2 tablespoons extra virgin olive oil

750 g (1½ lb) boneless shin of beef, cut into 2.5 cm (1 inch) cubes

1 large onion, chopped

2–3 garlic cloves, crushed

2 teaspoons ground cumin

2 teaspoons ground coriander

2–3 large red chillies, roasted, skinned, deseeded and finely chopped (see Tip)

1 bay leaf

1 sprig of thyme

2 large tomatoes, about 300 g (10 oz), skinned and chopped

600 ml (1 pint) beef stock

6 tablespoons chopped fresh coriander

salt

Cornmeal dumplings:

65 g (2½ oz) plain flour

75 g (3 oz) fine cornmeal

1½ teaspoons caster sugar

1 teaspoon baking powder

¼ teaspoon salt

100 ml (3½ fl oz) buttermilk, at room temperature

1 egg, beaten

25 g (1 oz) unsalted butter, melted

50 g (2 oz) canned sweetcorn kernels, drained

1. Boil the beans vigorously in a large saucepan of unsalted water for 10 minutes then drain.
2. Heat the oil in a large flameproof casserole. Add the meat in batches and brown well all over. Remove the browned meat with a slotted spoon and set aside.
3. Add the onion and garlic to the casserole and cook until the onion is golden brown, then add the cumin and ground coriander and cook for 1–2 minutes.
4. Add the drained beans, the meat and all the remaining ingredients except the fresh coriander and salt, and just enough water to cover – about 300 ml (½ pint). Bring to the boil, reduce the heat, cover tightly and simmer for 2–2½ hours until the meat is tender. Alternatively, cook in a preheated oven, 160°C (325°F), Gas Mark 3.
5. To make the dumplings, sift together the flour, cornmeal, sugar, baking powder and salt in a bowl. Add the buttermilk, egg and butter and stir until combined, then gently stir in the sweetcorn.
6. Stir the fresh coriander into the stew and season with salt. Drop 12 spoonfuls of the dumpling mixture over the stew, replace the lid and cook for 10–15 minutes until the dumplings are light and cooked. Serve hot.

TIP

To roast chillies, place them on a baking sheet and cook under a preheated grill for 5–10 minutes, turning occasionally until well charred and blistered all over. When cooked, remove from the heat and place in a plastic bag. Tie the top and leave the chillies to cool – the steam produced in the bag will help in removing the chilli skins. When cool enough to handle, peel off the skin and remove the pith and seeds. Chop the chilli flesh as required.

Serves 4 / Preparation time: 5 minutes / Cooking time: 1–1¼ hours

Chilli con Carne

One of Mexico's best-known dishes, this recipe combines beef, beans and fiery chillies to splendid effect.

2 tablespoons oil

3 onions, chopped

1 red pepper, cored, deseeded and diced

1 green pepper, cored, deseeded and diced

2 garlic cloves, crushed

500 g (1 lb) lean minced beef

450 ml (¾ pint) beef stock

¼–1 teaspoon chilli powder

475 g (15 oz) cooked kidney beans

425 g (14 oz) can chopped tomatoes

½ teaspoon ground cumin

salt and pepper

parsley, to garnish

To serve:

soft tortillas

soured cream

pickled green chillies

grated Cheddar cheese (optional)

1. Heat the oil in a heavy-bottomed saucepan or flameproof casserole. Add the onions, peppers and garlic and gently fry until soft. Add the meat and fry until just coloured. Blend in the stock and add the chilli powder, beans, tomatoes and cumin. Season with salt and pepper.

2. Bring to the boil, then cover, reduce the heat and simmer very gently for 50–60 minutes, stirring occasionally.

3. Serve the Chilli con Carne wrapped in soft tortillas, garnished with parsley and accompanied by the soured cream, green chillies and grated cheese, if liked.

4 Salads

Lobia Salad

Black-eyed beans feature in this unusual salad.

2 potatoes, finely diced

100 g (3½ oz) green beans, trimmed and cut into
   2.5 cm (1 inch) lengths

425 g (14 oz) can black-eyed beans, drained
   and rinsed

4 spring onions, thinly sliced

1 green chilli, deseeded and finely chopped

1 tomato, roughly chopped

handful of mint leaves

warm naan bread, to serve

Dressing:

2 tablespoons light olive oil

1 tablespoon lemon juice

½ teaspoon chilli powder

1 teaspoon clear honey

salt and pepper

1. Cook the potatoes and green beans in a large saucepan of lightly salted boiling water for 8–10 minutes. Drain and place in a large serving bowl.
2. Add the black-eyed beans, spring onions, green chilli, tomato and mint leaves. Toss well to mix.
3. Combine all the dressing ingredients in a small bowl or screw-top jar and mix well. Pour over the salad, mix well and serve with warm naan bread.

Rocket, Tuna and Haricot Bean Salad

4 tomatoes, skinned, cored and roughly chopped

125 g (4 oz) rocket

425 g (14 oz) can haricot beans, rinsed and drained

200 g (7 oz) can tuna in olive oil

1 red onion, chopped

125 g (4 oz) artichoke hearts in olive oil

2 young celery sticks with leaves, chopped

1 tablespoon pitted black olives

4 tablespoons lemon juice

1 tablespoon red wine vinegar

¼ teaspoon dried chilli flakes

handful of flat leaf parsley, roughly chopped

salt and pepper

warm crusty bread, to serve

1. Place the tomatoes in a large salad bowl with the rocket.

2. Stir in the haricot beans and the tuna and its olive oil, roughly breaking up the tuna into large flakes. Stir in the chopped red onion.

3. Add the artichoke hearts and their olive oil, the celery, olives, lemon juice, red wine vinegar, dried chilli flakes and parsley and season with salt and pepper.

4. Mix all the ingredients together well and allow to stand for 30 minutes for the flavours to mingle. Serve at room temperature with warm crusty bread.

Serves 4 / Preparation time: 10 minutes / Cooking time: 2 minutes

Tomato and Green Bean Salad

250 g (8 oz) mixed red and yellow baby
　tomatoes (plum tomatoes if possible)
250 g (8 oz) thin green beans, trimmed
handful of mint, chopped
1 garlic clove, crushed
4 tablespoons extra virgin olive oil
1 tablespoon balsamic vinegar
salt and pepper

1. Cut the baby tomatoes in half and place
   in a large bowl.
2. Blanch the green beans in a saucepan of
   lightly salted boiling water for 2 minutes,
   then drain well and place in the bowl
   with the tomatoes.
3. Add the chopped mint, garlic, olive oil
   and balsamic vinegar. Season with salt
   and pepper and mix well. Serve warm
   or cold.

FOOD FACT

Balsamic vinegar is a dark brown, rich,
concentrated, sweet vinegar made from the
must of white grapes. Traditionally from Modena
in Italy, true balsamic vinegar is aged in wooden
barrels and can be quite expensive. Use it
sparingly in salads or in cooking.

Serves 4 / Preparation time: 10 minutes / Cooking time: 2 minutes

White Bean and Sun-dried Tomato Salad

2 tablespoons olive oil

1 garlic clove, crushed

425 g (14 oz) can cannellini beans, drained and rinsed

1 red onion, sliced

125 g (4 oz) sun-dried tomatoes in oil, drained and roughly chopped

1 tablespoon chopped black olives

2 teaspoons chopped capers

2 teaspoons chopped thyme

1 tablespoon parsley leaves

1 tablespoon extra virgin olive oil

2 tablespoons lemon juice

salt and pepper

1. Heat the oil in a frying pan. Add the garlic and sauté over a high heat, stirring, to gain a little colour. When it is golden, remove from the pan.
2. Place the beans in a mixing bowl and stir in the garlic. Add the onion, sun-dried tomatoes, olives, capers, thyme, parsley, extra virgin olive oil, lemon juice and salt and pepper to taste; mix well. Check the seasoning and serve.

FOOD FACT

Capers are the small, green, unopened flower buds of a Mediterranean shrub. They are used, pickled, as a flavouring and as a garnish and are an essential ingredient in both Italian and Provençal cooking. They have a characteristic and slightly bitter flavour, which is developed by pickling.

New Season Broad Bean and Pecorino Salad

375 g (12 oz) shelled fresh broad beans

175 g (6 oz) pecorino cheese, coarsely grated

2 tablespoons extra virgin olive oil

2 tablespoons lemon juice

1 tablespoon chopped flat leaf parsley

salt and pepper

1. Blanch the beans in a saucepan of lightly salted boiling water for 2 minutes. Drain, rinse immediately under cold running water and drain again. If you have the time after blanching the beans carefully peel away and discard the rather tough outer skins to reveal the bright green, velvety bean inside.

2. Place the pecorino in a mixing bowl. Add the beans, olive oil, lemon juice and parsley, season with salt and pepper and mix well.

Serves 4 / Preparation time: 10 minutes, plus overnight soaking and standing / Cooking time: 45 minutes / Oven temperature: 160°C (325°F), Gas Mark 3

Cannellini Bean Salad

White, kidney-shaped cannellini beans feature in central Italian cooking, whereas rosy borlotti beans tend to appear in recipes from northern and southern Italy. The flavour is at its height if the beans are tossed while hot and eaten while still warm, so try to time the cooking of the beans so that they can stand for 1 hour between dressing and serving. For the best flavour and texture, buy Italian beans from a good Italian food shop.

200 g (7 oz) dried cannellini beans, soaked
    overnight, drained and rinsed

3 tablespoons extra virgin olive oil

2–3 anchovy fillets, rinsed if necessary

yolks of 2 hard-boiled eggs

2 tablespoons coarsely chopped onion

1 tablespoon white wine vinegar or lemon juice

3 sage leaves

2 tablespoons coarsely chopped parsley

salt and pepper

1. Place the beans in a heavy-bottomed flameproof casserole with just enough water to cover. Bring to the boil then cook over a medium heat for 10 minutes; cover and cook in a preheated oven, 160°C (325°F), Gas Mark 3, for 30 minutes, until tender. Keep an eye on the level of the water and pour in a little more if the beans become too dry, but there should be hardly any left at the end of the cooking.

2. Purée the olive oil, anchovies, egg yolks, onion, vinegar or lemon juice, herbs, salt and pepper in a blender or food processor.

3. Drain the cannellini beans and tip them into a large bowl. Pour over the dressing and toss gently until the beans are well coated. Leave at room temperature for 1 hour, then toss again just before serving.

VARIATION

Tuscan *Fagioli all'Uccelletto*: Cook 325 g (11 oz) soaked and drained cannellini beans as above. Fry 5 sage leaves and 2 crushed garlic cloves in 3 tablespoons extra virgin olive oil in a shallow earthenware dish until the garlic begins to colour. Stir in the beans and cook for about 5 minutes before adding 500 g (1 lb) well-flavoured tomatoes, skinned, deseeded and chopped, and salt and pepper. Cover and cook over a moderate heat for about 20 minutes.

Serves 4 / Preparation time: 15 minutes /
Cooking time: 40 minutes / Oven temperature: 200°C (400°F), Gas Mark 6

Flageolet Bean and Roasted Vegetable Salad

1 aubergine, trimmed

1 red pepper, halved, cored and deseeded

1 yellow pepper, halved, cored and deseeded

1 courgette, trimmed

4 garlic cloves, peeled but left whole

4 tablespoons extra virgin olive oil

1 teaspoon coarse sea salt

300 g (10 oz) cooked flageolet beans

2 tablespoons chopped mixed herbs (such as
    parsley and oregano or coriander and mint)

6 tablespoons French dressing

pepper

mint leaves, to garnish

1. Cut all the vegetables into strips and place in a roasting tin. Add the garlic cloves. Sprinkle over the olive oil, sea salt and pepper.

2. Place in a preheated oven, 200°C (400°F), Gas Mark 6, and roast for 40 minutes. Transfer to a shallow bowl and leave to cool.

3. Add the beans and toss lightly. Stir the herbs into the French dressing; pour over the salad and serve garnished with mint.

Bean and Rice Salad

75 g (3 oz) dried red kidney beans, soaked
    overnight, drained and rinsed

50 g (2 oz) dried cannellini beans, soaked
    overnight, drained and rinsed

175 g (6 oz) brown rice

2 spring onions, finely chopped

50 g (2 oz) raisins

50 g (2 oz) cashew nuts, roasted

½ red pepper, cored, deseeded and cut
    into diamonds

2 tablespoons chopped parsley

salt and pepper

lemon wedges, to serve

sprigs of flat leaf parsley, to garnish

Dressing:

75 ml (3 fl oz) sunflower oil

2 tablespoons soy sauce

1 tablespoon lemon juice

1 garlic clove, crushed

salt and pepper

1. Place the kidney beans and the cannellini beans separately in 2 large saucepans with plenty of cold water. Bring to the boil over a high heat and boil for 15 minutes. Reduce the heat, cover and simmer for 1–1½ hours adding a little salt towards the end of cooking. Drain and cool.

2. Meanwhile, cook the rice in a saucepan of lightly salted boiling water for 40–45 minutes until tender. Rinse, drain well and allow to cool.

3. Place the beans and rice in a large mixing bowl and stir in the spring onions, raisins, nuts, red pepper and parsley. Season with salt and pepper to taste.

4. Place all the dressing ingredients in a screw-top jar and shake well until blended. Season with salt and pepper. Pour over the rice and beans and stir well.

5. Transfer to a serving bowl and serve with lemon wedges and sprigs of parsley.

Serves 4 / Preparation time: 10 minutes, plus cooling / Cooking time: 10 minutes

Marinated Courgette and Bean Salad

250 g (8 oz) green beans, trimmed and cut into
   2.5 cm (1 inch) lengths

375 g (12 oz) courgettes, diced

475 g (15 oz) canned black-eyed beans, drained
   and rinsed

2 tablespoons extra virgin olive oil

2 tablespoons lemon juice

1 garlic clove, crushed

2 tablespoons chopped parsley

salt and pepper

toasted slices of crusty bread, to serve (optional)

1. Cook the green beans in a large saucepan of lightly salted boiling water for 5 minutes. Add the courgettes and cook for a further 5 minutes. Drain thoroughly and place in a bowl with the black-eyed beans.

2. Add the remaining ingredients, with salt and pepper to taste, while the vegetables are warm and mix well to combine. Leave to cool and serve with toasted slices of crusty bread, if liked.

Serves 4 / Preparation time: 10 minutes / Cooking time: 11 minutes

Smoked Tuna and Bean Salad

Smoked tuna is available in cans from most large supermarkets. The more traditional canned tuna can be used, but buy tuna packed in olive oil.

250 g (8 oz) baby new potatoes

125 g (4 oz) fine green beans, trimmed

2 x 125 g (4 oz) cans smoked tuna in olive oil, drained and flaked

425 g (14 oz) can borlotti beans or haricot beans, drained and rinsed

4 ripe plum tomatoes, roughly chopped

50 g (2 oz) Niçoise olives

2 tablespoons capers in brine, drained and rinsed

Dressing:

2 sun-dried tomatoes in oil, drained and roughly chopped

1 small garlic clove, crushed

½ teaspoon dried oregano

1 tablespoon white wine vinegar

pinch of sugar

6 tablespoons extra virgin olive oil

salt and pepper

1. Cook the potatoes in a saucepan of lightly salted boiling water for 8 minutes. Add the green beans and cook for a further 3 minutes, until both the potatoes and beans are tender. Drain, rinse immediately under cold running water and drain again, then pat dry and place in a large bowl.

2. Add the tuna, canned beans, tomatoes, olives and capers to the bowl.

3. To make the dressing, put the sun-dried tomatoes, garlic, oregano, vinegar, sugar and olive oil in a blender or food processor and process to a purée. Season to taste with salt and pepper. Pour the dressing over the salad, toss well and serve.

5 More Than Beans

Green Lentil Soup with Spiced Butter

Serve the spicy butter separately for stirring into the soup, so that each person can spice up their own portion according to personal taste.

2 tablespoons extra virgin olive oil

2 onions, chopped

2 bay leaves

175 g (6 oz) green lentils, rinsed

1 litre (1¾ pints) Vegetable Stock (see page 21)

½ teaspoon ground turmeric

small handful of coriander leaves, roughly
   chopped

salt and pepper

Spiced butter:

50 g (2 oz) lightly salted butter, softened

1 large garlic clove, crushed

1 tablespoon chopped coriander

1 teaspoon paprika

1 teaspoon cumin seeds

1 red chilli, deseeded and finely chopped

1. Heat the oil in a saucepan. Add the onions and sauté for 3 minutes. Add the bay leaves, lentils, vegetable stock and turmeric. Bring to the boil, then reduce the heat, cover and simmer for 20 minutes, or until the lentils are tender and turning mushy.

2. Meanwhile, to make the spiced butter, beat the butter with the garlic, coriander, paprika, cumin seeds and chilli and transfer to a small serving dish.

3. Stir the coriander leaves into the soup, season to taste with salt and pepper, and serve with the spiced butter in a separate bowl at the table for stirring into the soup.

Chickpea Soup

Instead of serving this as a chunky soup, it can
be puréed and served with a little extra virgin
olive oil swirled into each serving.

4 tablespoons extra virgin olive oil

1 onion, chopped

3 garlic cloves, crushed

1 tablespoon paprika

1 tablespoon ground coriander

2 teaspoons ground cumin

2 sprigs of thyme

pinch of dried chilli flakes

250 g (8 oz) dried chickpeas, soaked overnight,
    drained and rinsed

1.5 litres (2½ pints) Vegetable Stock (see page 21)

1 large potato, chopped

2 carrots, sliced

2 celery sticks, sliced

3 tomatoes, chopped

3 tablespoons chopped fresh coriander, plus
    extra to garnish

salt and pepper

1. Heat the oil in a saucepan. Add the onion and garlic and fry for 5–7 minutes until softened and beginning to brown. Add the paprika, ground coriander and cumin and stir for 2 minutes.
2. Add the thyme, dried chilli flakes, chickpeas and vegetable stock. Bring to the boil then cover the pan and simmer the soup for 40 minutes.
3. Add the potato, carrots, celery, tomatoes and fresh coriander to the pan. Cover and simmer for a further 30–40 minutes until the chickpeas and vegetables are tender.
4. Season to taste and serve with more fresh coriander scattered over the top.

Split Pea Soup

425 g (14 oz) yellow or green split peas, rinsed

1 large onion, chopped

2 garlic cloves, crushed

3 large sprigs of mint

3 tablespoons extra virgin olive oil

salt and pepper

Spiced butter:

2 garlic cloves, crushed

2 spring onions, finely chopped

1 teaspoon ground coriander

small pinch of dried chilli flakes

small handful of coriander leaves, chopped

2 tablespoons chopped mint

50 g (2 oz) unsalted butter

FOOD FACT

Split peas are usually yellow or green. They do not require soaking before use and easily cook to a purée (green split peas cooked to a purée are the basis of the traditional English dish, pease pudding). Ham or gammon is a classic partner for split peas in cooking.

1. Place the split peas, onion, garlic, sprigs of mint and olive oil in a large saucepan. Add sufficient water to cover generously and bring to the boil.

2. Reduce the heat, cover the pan and simmer for about 35 minutes, or until the split peas are very tender. Remove the lid towards the end of cooking if necessary – the split peas should be just covered with water.

3. Meanwhile, make the spiced butter. Place all the ingredients for the butter in a bowl and crush to a paste. Cover and store in the refrigerator until required.

4. Transfer two-thirds of the split peas and their liquid to a blender or food processor, purée until smooth then return to the pan. Simmer for a few minutes until thickened to the required consistency, then season to taste with salt and pepper.

5. Serve the soup in warmed bowls with a knob of the spiced butter floating on top.

Serves 6 / Preparation time: 15–20 minutes, plus overnight soaking / Cooking time: about 1¼ hours

Lamb Soup with Chickpeas and Couscous

1½ teaspoons cumin seeds

1½ teaspoons coriander seeds

2 tablespoons extra virgin olive oil

175 g (6 oz) lean lamb, finely chopped

1 large onion, chopped

3 garlic cloves, crushed

1 red chilli, deseeded and finely chopped

1½ teaspoons ground allspice

875 g (1¾ lb) canned chopped tomatoes

2 tablespoons tomato purée

900 ml (1½ pints) Vegetable Stock (see page 21)

125 g (4 oz) dried chickpeas, soaked overnight, drained and rinsed

2 tablespoons chopped parsley

1 tablespoon chopped mint

50 g (2 oz) couscous

about 2 teaspoons sugar

salt and pepper

lemon wedges, to serve

1. Place the cumin and coriander seeds in a small, heavy-bottomed frying pan and dry-fry over a moderate heat, stirring, for 1–2 minutes until fragrant – do not let them burn. Leave to cool, then grind to a powder in a spice grinder or using a pestle and mortar. Alternatively, put them into a small bowl and crush them with the end of a rolling pin. Set aside.

2. Heat the oil in a large heavy-bottomed saucepan. Add the lamb to the pan and brown quickly. Using a slotted spoon, remove the lamb and place on kitchen paper to drain. Stir the onion into the pan and cook until soft and browned, adding the garlic and chilli when the onion is almost cooked.

3. Add the dry-roasted and crushed cumin and coriander seeds and the allspice and stir for 1 minute.

4. Return the lamb to the pan and add the canned tomatoes, tomato purée, stock and chickpeas. Stir well then cover the pan and simmer very gently for about 1 hour until the chickpeas are tender.

5. Stir the parsley, mint and couscous into the soup, cover and remove from the heat. Add the sugar and salt and pepper to taste. Serve accompanied by lemon wedges.

Lentil, Aubergine and Coconut Dhal

This creamy, mildly spiced dhal makes a delicious accompaniment to Indian curries.

175 g (6 oz) red split lentils, rinsed

1 teaspoon ground turmeric

2 cinnamon sticks

750 ml (1¼ pints) hot Vegetable Stock
  (see page 21)

4 tablespoons sunflower oil

4 red chillies, deseeded and chopped

2 garlic cloves, crushed

2 teaspoons fenugreek seeds

1 teaspoon yellow mustard seeds

1 large onion, chopped

1 aubergine, diced

2 teaspoons garam masala

2 tablespoons tomato purée

1 tablespoon lemon juice

50 g (2 oz) creamed coconut

2 tablespoons chopped fresh coriander

salt and pepper

To garnish:
natural yogurt
chopped fresh coriander

1. Place the lentils in a saucepan with the turmeric, cinnamon sticks and hot stock. Bring to the boil, cover and simmer for 35–40 minutes until the lentils are softened and most of the stock has been absorbed.

2. Meanwhile, heat 1 tablespoon of the oil in a frying pan. Add the chillies, garlic, fenugreek seeds and mustard seeds and fry for 5 minutes until golden. Remove from the pan and set aside, reserving a teaspoon of the spice mixture for garnish.

3. Add the remaining oil to the frying pan and fry the onion and aubergine for 10 minutes until golden.

4. Return the chilli mixture to the pan with the garam masala, lentils, tomato purée and lemon juice. Simmer for 5 minutes. Meanwhile, mix together the yogurt, fresh coriander and reserved spice mixture for the garnish.

5. Stir the creamed coconut into the dhal until melted and add the fresh coriander; season to taste and serve at once topped with a spoonful of the garnish.

Braised Lentils with Mushrooms and Gremolata

Gremolata is a blend of chopped garlic, parsley and lemon rind, which gives a delicious lift to soups and stews. Sprinkle it over before serving.

50 g (2 oz) butter
1 onion, chopped
2 celery sticks, sliced
2 carrots, sliced
175 g (6 oz) Puy lentils, rinsed
600 ml (1 pint) Vegetable Stock (see page 21)
250 ml (8 fl oz) dry white wine
2 bay leaves
2 tablespoons chopped thyme
3 tablespoons extra virgin olive oil
325 g (11 oz) mushrooms, sliced
salt and pepper

Gremolata:
2 tablespoons chopped parsley
finely grated rind of 1 lemon
2 garlic cloves, chopped

1. Melt the butter in a saucepan. Add the onion, celery and carrots and sauté for 3 minutes. Add the lentils, vegetable stock, wine, herbs and a little salt and pepper. Bring to the boil, then reduce the heat and simmer gently, uncovered, for about 20 minutes, or until the lentils are tender.
2. Meanwhile, mix together the ingredients for the gremolata.
3. Heat the oil in a frying pan. Add the mushrooms and sauté quickly for about 2 minutes until golden. Season lightly with salt and pepper.
4. Spoon the lentils on to 4 warmed serving plates, top with the mushrooms and serve, scattered with the gremolata.

Mushroom and Chickpea Curry with Aromatic Rice

50 g (2 oz) butter

1 onion, chopped

2 garlic cloves, crushed

2.5 cm (1 inch) piece of fresh root ginger, peeled and grated

250 g (8 oz) button mushrooms

2 tablespoons hot curry powder

1 teaspoon ground coriander

1 teaspoon ground cinnamon

½ teaspoon turmeric

375 g (12 oz) potatoes, diced

425 g (14 oz) can chickpeas, drained and rinsed

50 g (2 oz) cashew nuts, toasted and chopped (optional)

125 ml (4 fl oz) Greek yogurt

chopped fresh coriander

salt and pepper

Aromatic rice:

375 g (12 oz) long grain rice

12 dried curry leaves

3 cardamom pods, crushed

1 cinnamon stick, crushed

1 teaspoon salt

750 ml (1¼ pints) water

1. First cook the rice. Place the rice in a saucepan with the curry leaves, spices and salt. Add the water, bring to the boil, then cover and cook over a low heat for 10 minutes. Remove the pan from the heat, but leave the rice undisturbed for a further 10 minutes.

2. Meanwhile, melt the butter in a frying pan and fry the onion, garlic, ginger and mushrooms for 5 minutes.

3. Add the curry powder, ground coriander, cinnamon, turmeric and potatoes, stir, then add the chickpeas. Season to taste with salt and pepper and add just enough water to cover. Bring to the boil, cover and simmer gently for 15 minutes.

4. Stir the cashew nuts into the curry, if using, along with the yogurt and chopped fresh coriander. Heat through without boiling and serve with the rice.

Spinach and Chickpea Sabzi

This quick and tasty Indian dish uses spinach and canned chickpeas, flavoured with amchur (dried mango powder).

1 tablespoon vegetable oil

1 teaspoon cumin seeds

½ teaspoon coarsely ground coriander seeds

1 small onion, finely chopped

250 g (8 oz) baby spinach

200 g (7 oz) canned chopped tomatoes

1 teaspoon chilli powder

1 tablespoon dhana jeera

1 teaspoon amchur

1 teaspoon jaggery or soft brown sugar

1 tablespoon fresh lime juice

425 g (14 oz) can chickpeas, drained and rinsed

175 ml (6 fl oz) water

sea salt and pepper

1. Heat the oil in a large frying pan and, when hot, add the cumin and coriander seeds and the onion. Stir-fry until the onion is soft and light brown, then add the spinach and tomatoes and stir well.

2. Add the chilli powder, dhana jeera, amchur, jaggery or sugar and lime juice and stir. Cook for 1–2 minutes, then add the chickpeas and water. Season with salt and pepper, cover and simmer gently for 10 minutes, stirring occasionally. Serve hot.

FOOD FACT

Dhana jeera is a spice mixture comprising equal quantities of ground coriander and ground cumin.

Spicy Chickpeas

300 g (10 oz) dried chickpeas, soaked
   overnight, drained and rinsed

1½ teaspoons salt

1 whole onion, peeled, plus 2 onions, chopped

6 rashers of streaky bacon, chopped

1 garlic clove, crushed

1 red pepper, cored, deseeded and chopped

¼ teaspoon pepper

1 small dried hot red chilli, crumbled

½ teaspoon dried oregano

300 g (10 oz) tomatoes, skinned, deseeded
   and chopped

2 tablespoons tomato purée

100 ml (3½ fl oz) water

oregano leaves, to garnish

1. Place the chickpeas in a saucepan with 1 teaspoon of the salt and the whole onion. Cover with cold water.

2. Bring to the boil, then boil hard for 10 minutes. Reduce the heat and simmer, uncovered, for about 45 minutes, until the chickpeas are cooked and tender. Drain and set aside; discard the onion.

3. Place the bacon in a frying pan and fry until the fat starts to run out of the bacon. Add the 2 chopped onions, the garlic and red pepper and continue frying until soft. Stir in the remaining salt, the pepper, chilli, oregano, tomatoes, tomato purée and water.

4. Add the drained chickpeas and stir well. Simmer for 10 minutes, stirring occasionally. Serve hot, garnished with oregano leaves.

Hummus

The quantities for this delicious chickpea and sesame dip are imprecise because people's tastes vary considerably, but the flavour of sesame (the tahini) should not overpower that of the chickpeas.

FOOD FACT

Tahini, or tahina, is a thick oily, light or dark brown paste made from ground, toasted sesame seeds. It is widely used in Middle Eastern cuisine. Tahini separates on standing so stir it well before use.

250 g (8 oz) dried chickpeas, soaked overnight, drained and rinsed
2–3 garlic cloves, crushed with a little salt
about 250 ml (8 fl oz) lemon juice
about 5 tablespoons tahini
salt
warm pitta bread, to serve

To garnish:
extra virgin olive oil
paprika
olives

1. Cook the chickpeas in a large saucepan of boiling water until soft – 1–1½ hours depending on their quality and age. Drain and reserve the cooking liquid. Purée the chickpeas in a blender or food processor with a little of the cooking liquid, then press the purée through a sieve to remove the skins.

2. Beat the garlic into the chickpea purée. Stir in the lemon juice and tahini alternately, tasting before it has all been added to get the right balance of flavours. Add a little more salt, if necessary, and more of the cooking liquid to make a soft, creamy consistency. Spoon the purée into a shallow dish, cover and leave in the refrigerator for several hours.

3. Return to room temperature before serving. Create swirls in the surface with the back of a spoon then trickle olive oil into the swirls and sprinkle lightly with paprika. Garnish with olives and serve with warm pitta bread.

Serves 4 / Preparation time: 35 minutes, plus overnight soaking / Cooking time: 1–1½ hours

Chickpea, Spinach and Pumpkin Stew with Tomato and Chilli Aïoli

375 g (12 oz) dried chickpeas, soaked
   overnight, drained and rinsed

2 tablespoons extra virgin olive oil

1 onion, finely chopped

1 garlic clove, finely chopped

500 g (1 lb) peeled pumpkin, cut into 2.5 cm
   (1 inch) dice

500 ml (17 fl oz) Vegetable Stock (see page 21)

1 bay leaf

pinch of saffron threads

500 g (1 lb) fresh spinach, washed and trimmed

1 tablespoon cider or white wine vinegar

salt and pepper

Tomato and chilli aïoli:

4–6 garlic cloves, crushed

2 egg yolks

1 red chilli, roasted, skinned, deseeded and
   chopped (see page 90)

2–4 tablespoons lemon juice

300 ml (½ pint) extra virgin olive oil

1 tablespoon sun-dried tomato purée

salt and pepper

1. Place the chickpeas in a large saucepan with sufficient water to cover – about 1.2 litres (2 pints). Bring to the boil, reduce the heat and simmer for ¾–1 hour, or until tender. Drain and set aside.

2. Meanwhile, to make the aïoli, place the garlic, egg yolks and chilli in a blender or food processor, add 2 tablespoons of the lemon juice and process briefly to mix. With the motor running, gradually add the olive oil in a thin steady stream (as if making mayonnaise), until the mixture forms a thick cream. Scrape into a serving bowl and season to taste with salt, pepper and more lemon juice if required. Stir in the sun-dried tomato purée and set aside.

3. Heat the oil in a large flameproof casserole over a moderate heat. Add the onion and garlic and cook for 6–8 minutes until softened and lightly golden. Add the pumpkin, stock, bay leaf, saffron and chickpeas. Season, bring to the boil, reduce the heat and simmer for 10–15 minutes until the pumpkin is tender.

4. Stir in the spinach, cover and cook, stirring occasionally, until the spinach has just wilted. Stir in the vinegar and adjust the seasoning to taste. Serve in large individual bowls and hand round the aïoli to stir into each portion.

Tarka Dhal

This is the ultimate basic Indian comfort food. Tarka is the process by which food is given the final seasoning, in this case with spiced oil, to flavour the dish. This dhal is tasty served with basmati rice, natural yogurt and hot green mango pickle or lime pickle.

250 g (8 oz) red split lentils, rinsed
1 litre (1¾ pints) hot water
200 g (7 oz) canned chopped tomatoes
2 green chillies, deseeded and finely
   chopped (optional)
¼ teaspoon ground turmeric
2 teaspoons grated fresh root ginger
4 tablespoons chopped fresh coriander
sea salt and pepper

Tarka:

1 tablespoon sunflower oil
2 teaspoons black mustard seeds
1 teaspoon cumin seeds
2 garlic cloves, thinly sliced
1 dried red chilli

1. Soak the lentils in sufficient boiling water to cover for 10 minutes. Drain and put in a large saucepan with the measured hot water. Bring to the boil over a high heat, spooning off the scum that comes to the surface. Reduce the heat and cook for 20 minutes, or until soft and tender.
2. Drain the lentils and process to a purée in a blender or food processor or using a hand-held electric whisk. Return the purée to the rinsed pan with the tomatoes, chillies, if using, turmeric, ginger and fresh coriander. Season with salt and pepper, return to the heat and simmer gently.
3. Meanwhile, make the tarka. Heat the oil in a smooth nonstick frying pan. When hot, add all the tarka ingredients and fry, stirring constantly, for 1–2 minutes.
4. Remove the tarka from the heat and pour on to the cooked dhal. Stir and serve hot.

Chickpea Purée with Eggs and Spiced Oil

Smooth chickpea purée, topped with fried eggs and spicy oil, makes a great snack at any time of the day. Serve any leftover purée with warm pitta bread, just as you would hummus.

425 g (14 oz) can chickpeas, drained and rinsed

3 garlic cloves, sliced

4 tablespoons tahini

4 tablespoons milk

5 tablespoons extra virgin olive oil

4 tablespoons lemon juice

2 eggs

½ teaspoon each of cumin, coriander and fennel seeds, lightly crushed

1 teaspoon sesame seeds

¼ teaspoon dried chilli flakes

good pinch of ground turmeric

salt and pepper

fresh coriander leaves, to garnish

1. Place the chickpeas in a blender or food processor with the garlic, tahini, milk, 2 tablespoons of the oil and 3 tablespoons of the lemon juice. Season to taste with salt and pepper and process until smooth, scraping the mixture from around the sides of the bowl halfway through. Transfer to a small heavy-bottomed saucepan and heat through gently for about 3 minutes while preparing the eggs.

2. Heat another tablespoon of the oil in a small frying pan and fry the eggs. Pile the chickpea purée on to 2 warmed serving plates and top each mound with an egg.

3. Add the remaining oil and spices to the pan and heat through gently for 1 minute. Season lightly with salt and pepper and stir in the remaining lemon juice. Pour over the eggs and serve garnished with fresh coriander leaves.

Middle Eastern Beef Casserole with Chickpeas and Courgettes

3 tablespoons extra virgin olive oil

1.5 kg (3 lb) stewing beef, cut into 3.5 cm
   (1½ inch) cubes

2 onions, sliced

2 garlic cloves, chopped

375 g (12 oz) tomatoes, skinned and chopped

1 tablespoon tomato purée

1 teaspoon ground allspice

175 g (6 oz) dried chickpeas, soaked overnight,
   drained and rinsed

900 ml (1½ pints) water

cayenne pepper

750 g (1½ lb) courgettes, sliced

25 g (1 oz) flat leaf parsley, chopped

salt and pepper

bulgar wheat, to serve

1. Heat the oil in a large flameproof casserole over a moderate heat. Add the meat, in batches, and brown well all over. Remove the browned meat using a slotted spoon and set aside.

2. Reduce the heat under the casserole, add the onions and garlic and cook for 5–6 minutes until softened. Return the meat to the pan and add the tomatoes, tomato purée, allspice and chickpeas. Cover with the water, stir well and bring to the boil. Season with salt, pepper and cayenne pepper.

3. Reduce the heat, cover with a tight-fitting lid and simmer gently for 1½ hours. Add the courgettes and half of the parsley and cook for a further 15–20 minutes, stirring occasionally, until the meat is tender and the chickpeas are cooked. Stir in the remaining parsley and serve with bulgar wheat.

FOOD FACT

Bulgar wheat, also known as cracked wheat and burghul, is a staple grain eaten throughout the Middle East. Already parboiled then dried and ground, bulgar is therefore quick to cook. It has a light texture and nutty taste. It is probably best known as the main ingredient of the Lebanese salad, tabbouleh, where it is combined with onions, parsley and mint.

North African Fish Stew with Couscous

125 g (4 oz) dried chickpeas, soaked overnight, drained and rinsed

2 onions, peeled

4 tablespoons extra virgin olive oil

1–2 garlic cloves, sliced

1 celery stick, sliced

1 red or green pepper, cored, deseeded and cut into strips

1 teaspoon Harissa (see page 20)

1 teaspoon ground cumin

375 g (12 oz) ripe tomatoes, skinned and chopped

1 tablespoon tomato purée

2 carrots, sliced

large pinch of saffron threads

1.2 litres (2 pints) fish or chicken stock

500 g (1 lb) instant couscous

1–1.25 kg (2–2½ lb) firm white fish (such as bass, mullet, bream, snapper, cod), scaled, gutted and cut into large pieces

1½ tablespoons chopped parsley

1½ tablespoons chopped fresh coriander

salt and pepper

1. Place the chickpeas in a saucepan and cover with water. Bring to the boil, reduce the heat and simmer for about 1 hour, or until tender. Drain.

2. Cut the onions into wedges, keeping the root ends intact so that the layers do not separate. Heat the oil in a large flameproof casserole, add the onion wedges, garlic and celery and cook for 10–12 minutes until softened and golden. Add the pepper, harissa and ground cumin and cook for 5 minutes. Add the tomatoes, tomato purée, carrots, saffron, stock and drained chickpeas. Bring to the boil, reduce the heat and simmer gently for 15 minutes. Season to taste.

3. Meanwhile, cook the couscous according to the packet instructions and keep warm.

4. Add the fish pieces to the stew and cook for 5 minutes, or until they are opaque. Stir in the herbs. Spoon the stew over the couscous, to serve.

Rice and Lentil Pilaff

One-pot recipes like this one are a feature of the traditional cooking of Morocco, Algeria and Tunisia, where it was more practical to use the minimum number of cooking pots.

2 tablespoons extra virgin olive oil

1 onion, finely chopped

4 garlic cloves, crushed

2 carrots, chopped

1 small aubergine, cubed

1 teaspoon ground ginger

1 teaspoon paprika

1 teaspoon ground coriander

1 teaspoon ground cumin

250 g (8 oz) red lentils, rinsed

250 g (8 oz) white long grain rice

1 litre (1¾ pints) Vegetable Stock (see page 21)

250 g (8 oz) spinach, washed and shredded

2 tablespoons sesame seeds, lightly toasted

salt and pepper

1. Heat the oil in a large heavy-bottomed saucepan. Add the onion, garlic, carrots and aubergine and fry for 5 minutes, stirring occasionally.

2. Stir the ginger, paprika, coriander and cumin into the pan and cook, stirring, for 1 minute then stir in the lentils and rice. When well mixed, add the stock. Bring to the boil, cover the pan and simmer gently, stirring occasionally, for 30–35 minutes until the rice and lentils are tender and the stock has been absorbed.

3. Stir in the spinach and cook for 2 minutes until it has thoroughly wilted. Season to taste with salt and pepper and scatter with the sesame seeds.

Serves 4 / Preparation time: 10 minutes / Cooking time: 25 minutes

Gammon Steaks with Creamy Lentils

125 g (4 oz) Puy lentils, rinsed

50 g (2 oz) butter

2 shallots

1 garlic clove, chopped

2 sprigs of thyme, crushed

1 teaspoon cumin seeds

4 teaspoons Dijon mustard

2 teaspoons clear honey

4 gammon steaks

125 ml (4 fl oz) dry cider

75 ml (3 fl oz) single cream

salt and pepper

thyme leaves, to garnish

1. Place the lentils in a saucepan and cover with cold water. Bring to the boil and cook for 20 minutes.

2. Meanwhile, melt the butter in a frying pan and fry the shallots, garlic, thyme and cumin seeds, stirring frequently, for 10 minutes, until the shallots are soft and golden.

3. Blend the mustard and honey together and season to taste with salt and pepper. Brush the mixture over the gammon steaks and grill them for 3 minutes on each side, until golden and cooked through. Keep warm.

4. Drain the lentils and add them to the shallot mixture. Pour in the cider, bring to the boil and cook until reduced to about 4 tablespoons. Stir in the cream, heat through and season to taste with salt and pepper. Serve the lentils with the gammon steaks, garnished with thyme leaves.

Serves 4 / Preparation time: 20 minutes, plus overnight soaking / Cooking time: 1½ hours

Chicken Tagine with Rice and Chickpeas

125 g (4 oz) dried chickpeas, soaked overnight, drained and rinsed

4 tablespoons lemon juice

pinch of crushed saffron threads

2 tablespoons extra virgin olive oil

4 chicken leg joints

2 large onions, chopped

2 large red peppers, cored, deseeded and thickly sliced lengthways

3 garlic cloves, crushed

1 red chilli, deseeded and finely chopped

1½ teaspoons ground cumin

1½ teaspoons ground coriander

stalks from a bunch of coriander, chopped

1 ripe thin-skinned lemon, thinly sliced

175 g (6 oz) white long grain rice

450 ml (¾ pint) chicken stock

125 g (4 oz) mixed pitted green and black olives

salt and pepper

1. Cook the chickpeas in a saucepan of boiling water for 20 minutes. Drain.

2. Meanwhile, put the lemon juice into a small bowl, add the saffron threads and leave to soak.

3. Heat the oil in a heavy-bottomed flameproof casserole. Add the chicken joints and brown quickly. Remove from the casserole and place on kitchen paper to drain. Add the onions and red peppers to the pan and cook over a high heat, stirring frequently, until browned. Reduce the heat and stir in the garlic, chilli, cumin, ground coriander and fresh coriander stalks, lemon slices, rice, chickpeas, saffron liquid and chicken stock. Return the chicken to the casserole, heat to simmering point then cover and cook very gently for 30 minutes.

4. Scatter the olives over the casserole and push them into the liquid. Cover the casserole and cook for a further 30 minutes until the chicken is cooked and the chickpeas and rice are tender. Season to taste and serve hot.

Serves 4 / Preparation time: 10 minutes

Couscous, Chickpea and Prawn Salad

This easily made salad offers an interesting combination of textures and flavours.

175 g (6 oz) cooked couscous
425 g (14 oz) can chickpeas, drained and rinsed
500 g (1 lb) cooked peeled prawns
2 spring onions, thinly sliced
3 well-flavoured tomatoes, deseeded
   and chopped
bunch of mint, chopped
lemon wedges, to serve

Dressing:
6 tablespoons extra virgin olive oil
3 tablespoons lemon juice
pinch of caster sugar
paprika
salt and pepper

1. To make the dressing, whisk together the oil and lemon juice in a small bowl or shake them together well in a screw-top jar. Add the sugar, paprika and salt and pepper to taste.
2. Mix the couscous with the chickpeas, prawns, spring onions, tomatoes and mint. Pour over the dressing and toss well to coat all the ingredients. Serve with lemon wedges.

Serves 4–6 / Preparation time: 10 minutes

Fast Chickpea Salad

Canned chickpeas are a great product as they retain their flavour and texture and do away with the lengthy soaking and cooking time that dried ones require. This is a simple salad with the Mediterranean flavours of olive oil, garlic, lemon and fresh parsley.

2 x 425 g (14 oz) cans chickpeas, drained
   and rinsed
6 spring onions, finely sliced
1 red chilli, deseeded and finely sliced
4 tablespoons chopped parsley
grilled pitta or other warm bread, to serve

Dressing:
6 tablespoons extra virgin olive oil
1–2 garlic cloves, crushed
½ teaspoon finely grated lemon rind
3 tablespoons lemon juice
salt and pepper

1. Place the chickpeas in a large serving bowl with the spring onions, chilli and parsley.
2. Whisk together the dressing ingredients in a small bowl or place them in a screw-top jar and shake well to combine. Pour the dressing over the salad and toss to mix. Serve the salad with grilled pitta or other warm bread.

Index

Acknowledgements

Executive Editor: Nicky Hill
Editor: Sharon Ashman
Senior Designer: Joanna Bennett
Production Controller: Jo Sim
Index compiled by Indexing Specialists

Special Photography: William Reavell
Food Stylist: Oona van den Berg

All other photography Octopus Publishing Group
 Limited/David Loftus 52, 84, 99/Ian Wallace
 25, 136/Neil Mersh 55, 106/Peter Myers
 83/Roger Stowell 73/Sandra Lane 107,
 122/Sean Myers 29, 60, 114, 123,
 141/Simon Smith 119